"The variety of perspectives gather___ ___r thinking, clarify your convictions, and pursue integrity and g___ as you seek healthy, mature Christian relationships."

—ALBERT Y. HSU
author of *Singles at the Crossroads*

"*5 Paths to the Love of Your Life* shows there is no 'one size fits all' in this adventure, and we are shown illuminating points of comparison and contrast among the options. This book details in clear language the ways serious believers may think about the paths to marriage."

—BEN PATTERSON
campus pastor, Westmont College, Santa Barbara, California

"Biblical, practical, contemporary. Those three words came to mind as I read *5 Paths to the Love of Your Life*. Pastors, youth workers, parents, and single adults will find it an invaluable resource on the difficult questions surrounding dating, courtship, and marriage in the twenty-first century. Get ready to have your thinking stretched and challenged."

—DR. RAY PRITCHARD
senior pastor; author of *An Anchor for Your Soul*,
Discovering God's Will for Your Life, and *He's God and We're Not*

"Dating is an issue of Christian controversy—and for good reason. This fascinating new book brings together some of the most important thinkers and writers on this issue, producing a dialogue that will stretch the mind and encourage Christian thinking. Read this book—it's sure to become a focus of much conversation."

—R. ALBERT MOHLER JR.

president, The Southern Baptist Theological Seminary, Louisville, Kentucky

"Recent books on courtship and dating have raised some difficult questions about the proper approach Christians should take for finding a life partner. This book lays out the major views and unpacks their scriptural arguments. If you're trying to understand all the views and think carefully through their biblical merit, here is the book you are looking for."

—JOHN MACARTHUR

pastor, Grace Community Church, Sun Valley, California;

president, The Master's College and Seminary

DEFINING YOUR DATING STYLE

5 PATHS TO THE LOVE OF YOUR LIFE

LAUREN F. WINNER | DOUGLAS WILSON | RICK HOLLAND

JONATHAN LINDVALL | JERAMY & JERUSHA CLARK

GENERAL EDITOR **ALEX CHEDIAK**

TH1NK
P.O. Box 35001
Colorado Springs, Colorado 80935

TH1NK is an imprint of NavPress.
TH1NK and the TH1NK logo are registered trademarks of NavPress. Absence of ®
in connection with marks of NavPress or other parties does not indicate an absence of
registration of those marks.

ISBN 1-57683-709-2

Cover design by Kirk DouPonce, DogEaredDesign.com
Cover photo by Malek Chamoun, Getty
Creative Team: Nicci Jordan, Arvid Wallen, Kathy Mosier, Glynese Northam

5 paths to the love of your life : defining your dating style / Lauren
F. Winner ... [et al.].
      p. cm.
   Includes bibliographical references.
   ISBN 1-57683-709-2
   1. Single people--Conduct of life. 2. Dating (Social
customs)--Religious aspects--Christianity. 3. Marriage--Religious
aspects--Christianity. I. Winner, Lauren F.
   BV4596.S5A15 2005
   241'.6765--dc22
                              2005016795

Printed in Canada

1 2 3 4 5 6 7 8 9 10 / 09 08 07 06 05

CONTENTS

ACKNOWLEDGMENTS   7
        Alex Chediak

INTRODUCTION TO THE 5 PATHS   9
        Alex Chediak

PATH
  1   THE COUNTERCULTURAL PATH   17
        Lauren F. Winner

  2   THE COURTSHIP PATH   57
        Douglas Wilson

  3   THE GUIDED PATH   89
        Rick Holland

  4   THE BETROTHAL PATH   123
        Jonathan Lindvall

  5   THE PURPOSEFUL PATH   153
        Jeramy & Jerusha Clark

CONCLUSION: HOW THIS ALL COMES TOGETHER   191
        Alex Chediak

APPENDIX: A BIRD'S-EYE VIEW OF THIS BOOK'S ORGANIZATION   201
        Alex Chediak

NOTES   207

AUTHORS   215

ACKNOWLEDGMENTS

Alex Chediak

INNUMERABLE FRIENDS AND MENTORS SHARED THOUGHTS WITH ME as I sought to integrate biblical wisdom with premarital romance. I think of Alan Perkins and Eric Larson in Vermont and Scott Harris in New York and of my interactions with Tim Wat, Bill Garaway, Joost Nixon, and Mike Lawyer. I am grateful for the conversations I had with Mark Dever, Al Mohler, and Andy Farmer at the Sovereign Grace Conference and the many "iron sharpening iron" interactions with Calvin Lu, Brett Warneke, Erik Chou, and countless others. I appreciate the brethren at Grace Community Church in Gardnerville, Nevada, particularly Brian Borgman, who gave me the opportunity to teach a series of messages on relationships over the summer of 2004.

I am thankful for the editorial assistance I received from Brent Parker, Eric Chi, Janet Balsiger, Vic and Berti Rice, Darren Parker, Andrew Cowan, Vicki Anderson, and Martha Kelley, particularly while trying to place this book but even afterward. The coaching I had from Pastor Ray Pritchard on working with publishers was invaluable and deeply honoring. I am grateful for the encouragement from Al Hsu and for his insight regarding the three relationship scenarios. I am thankful to Alex Strauch, who believed in this project and introduced me to Paul Santhouse, who led me to Dan Rich at NavPress, who in turn made this book happen. I am grateful to have worked with Nicci Jordan and Kathy Mosier—outstanding editors who kept this book focused and well structured.

Finally, I am profoundly indebted to my wife and best friend, Marni. I love you more deeply every day. Thank you for your steadfast devotion, love, and support. I am so excited for our life together.

INTRODUCTION TO THE 5 PATHS

Alex Chediak

MATT AND STACY LIKE EACH OTHER — A LOT. YOU KNOW HOW IT GOES. After some flirting and hinting, Matt finally asks Stacy out. But Stacy isn't sure what to do. Part of her wants to say yes because she'd like to get to know Matt better. But the thing is, Stacy's good friends Kent and Julie are influencing her otherwise. They've sworn off dating because of all the junk that goes with relationships, especially ones that break up. Apparently, both Kent and Julie were recently burned in a relationship.

Kent was completely "in love" with his girlfriend, Samantha, but she suddenly decided he wasn't the one for her, and she wanted to see other people. Julie and her boyfriend were getting along great until he got a bit too physical. Julie felt used. She had been wanting to feel close to him and loved by him, yet ironically, she felt anything but. Both couples broke up, leaving Kent and Julie bruised, battered, and determined to prevent this mess from ever happening again. They kissed dating good-bye and are encouraging Stacy to do the same. They suggest that instead of dating, Stacy should require Matt to do the "biblical" thing and approach her father for permission to see her, spend time with her only in groups, and follow the typical steps of courtship.

On the other hand, Stacy's best friend, Emily, is a huge proponent of dating. She's been assuring Stacy that the only way to know if Matt is right for her is to go out with him alone as a couple. Emily believes dating is a fun and innocent way to find "the one." She has experienced plenty of breakups but continues to date, hoping she'll find a diamond in the rough. Stacy knows, however, that Emily has given up quite a bit as far as sexuality is concerned, and she fears that if she's too quick to date Matt, she may end up compromising her purity as well.

Stacy is frustrated that falling in love, such a seemingly simple thing (at least in the movies), can be so complicated. She thinks, *I like Matt, but if dating is such a bad option, how in the world can I get to know him in a way that could lead to something permanent? But what happens if we get to know each other too well and then break up?* With these questions bouncing around in Stacy's mind, Matt continues to pursue her. Finally succumbing to her growing feelings for Matt, Stacy decides to go out with him. Confused, she thinks, *Would dating him really hurt? Does God actually have an answer on how this is supposed to work?*

This scenario is fictional, but the dilemmas it illustrates and the questions it raises are familiar to many Christian singles. The question, *If dating is okay, which I'm not sure it is, how do I date and still honor God?* has become important to single people everywhere. With the number of singles in America increasing each year,[1] interest in issues pertaining to dating and romance has likewise risen to unprecedented levels. Since Joshua Harris's instant bestseller *I Kissed Dating Goodbye*, a plethora of books have appeared, claiming a wide variety of approaches to finding a marriage partner.

Many of these books disagree with each other. Some argue that kissing dating good-bye is not the answer. Many Christians, after all, think dating is a great environment where you can learn more about your strengths, weaknesses, and preferences. They think you can fondly remember your first dates and high school dances without feeling hardened or embarrassed. Some maintain that rather than contributing to emotional baggage, breakup experiences can make you stronger and more prepared for marriage.

Others believe that the institution of dating is fundamentally flawed. From their perspective, no matter how careful you are to stay emotionally and physically pure, dating will still cause damage. The thought process goes something like this: If you succeed at staying pure, you learn a bad habit of guarding yourself in an environment where God intended you to be unabashedly open. Even if your relationship succeeds, this will make it harder for you to be emotionally vulnerable in marriage. And if your relationship ends, the breakup experience can harden your heart and make it easier for you to divorce when a future marriage becomes difficult.

Harris's book struck a chord for one simple reason: Deep down inside, many Christians are frustrated with their dating experiences. They've been wounded. They've given in to sexual temptation. They've compromised their standards to avoid being lonely. They know, instinctively, that it should not be this way. Most do not desire to position themselves for lifelong singleness, but very few know how to go about finding true, lasting, committed, exclusive love.

This book is here to help. Our goal is not to proselytize you to any particular position but instead to provide the big picture: the logic behind five of the most widespread perspectives on relationships held by Christians today (some more controversial than others, depending on your personal point of view). That way, you can make your own biblically informed decisions, being fully educated and, Lord willing, more mature and intentional about the way you approach relationships.

THE FIVE PATHS

We've selected top-notch representatives of each viewpoint to share their perspectives with you. This is what you'll read:

Chapter 1: **The Countercultural Path** — To date or not to date isn't the question for Lauren F. Winner. Instead, she suggests that dating can be a godly practice but, like many other Christian practices, should cut against the grain of typical American dating habits. She says dating can be godly when done within the context of community, chastity, love, and orientation toward marriage (although she does not claim that every dating relationship will or should end in marriage).

Chapter 2: **The Courtship Path** — Methods and principles only get you so far, Douglas Wilson says, but still, some methods are better than others. Douglas suggests the best principle is courtship, in which the head of the household holds the authority over a couple's relationship. Courtship is a serious business in which both parties are committed to pursuing marriage, although breaking up is acceptable under some circumstances.

Chapter 3: **The Guided Path** — Rick Holland provides ten principles he believes set the standard for a healthy relationship leading toward marriage. He suggests that dating, within the context of these ten principles, can be a godly way to find "the one," but only when marriage is a realistic and age-appropriate outcome. Casual dating is therefore inappropriate.

Chapter 4: **The Betrothal Path** — Dating not only is unacceptable, says Jonathan Lindvall, but also actually defrauds the other person (as does flirting). Jonathan suggests the only scripturally normative path to pursue a relationship is through betrothal, in which the couple enters a permanent commitment to marry one another at the start of their relationship. The relationship proceeds under the authority of the woman's father, and breaking up is unacceptable under any circumstances.

Chapter 5: **The Purposeful Path**—Dating doesn't have to be serious, claim Jeramy and Jerusha Clark, but it does need to be taken seriously. Based on the belief that dating can be a fun and godly way to get to know members of the opposite sex, the Clarks suggest general guidelines for going about a dating relationship with the purpose of personal and spiritual refinement. As men and women date purposefully, they will be shaped into more godly individuals better able to relate to the opposite sex and well prepared for the adventure and crucible of marriage.

THE STRUCTURE

Each chapter will focus on one perspective. Within each chapter, the authors will provide:

- The key definition and distinctives of their perspective

- The reasons they hold their opinions

- Key scriptural and spiritual implications

- The benefits of their approach

- Potential weaknesses of their approach

- An overview of their approach and some helpful suggestions for practicing it

Additionally, I've asked each author to address the scenarios that follow for a couple of reasons. First, each of these scenarios is common among Christians, so it will turn the conversation to where the rubber meets the road. Second, it will further clarify each author's approach by looking at common scenarios from different points of view.

Though the contributors will be highlighting their differences, they do possess a common foundation. Each is a Christian and thus understands the Bible to be authoritative for matters of faith and practice. Consequently, each author holds marriage in high honor and is convinced that sexual activity outside of marriage is both contrary to God's will and with God's help can be avoided (see Hebrews 13:4; 1 Thessalonians 4:3). The contributors also maintain that a Christian should not marry a non-Christian (see 2 Corinthians 6:14).

THE SCENARIOS

Scenario 1: Jenny and David are high school juniors in the same church youth group. Both come from Christian families and have involved, caring Christian parents. Their friends have told them they'd make a cute couple. They're really social and have group-dated a lot but have never spent time dating one-on-one. What should they do, if anything?

Scenario 2: Steve and Rachel are college students at a state university. Steve became a Christian in high school; Rachel just became a Christian through friends in a campus ministry. Neither of their families is Christian. They are very attracted to each other. How should they proceed, if at all?

Scenario 3: Denise just turned thirty. She is a business professional working in a big city across the country from her parents. She is active in her local church and busy with friends and activities but has not had any real experience with romantic relationships. Like many women her age, she feels her biological clock ticking and wants to get married and have children. What would you advise her to do, if anything?

THE ROLE OF SCRIPTURE

If the Bible is our guide for living, then interpreting the Bible and applying it are of paramount importance. So it is really a question of hermeneutics—a big word that simply refers to the rules we use to determine what the Bible means. It is not news that Christians who are committed to Scripture disagree on many of the things it says. Depending on the rules used, it can be interpreted differently. And that's one reason the right way to conduct Christian relationships is a disputable matter.

YOUR OWN PERSONAL DATING STYLE

So now that you've got the scoop, read on! As you read, you'll probably find yourself both nodding and glaring at the book in your hands. But, overall, I'm confident you'll find this book helpful, confirming, and probably even motivating. As you read, try to appreciate the strengths of each of the views. Even if you don't agree, ask yourself, *Why might someone want to practice that?* Or, *How can this help me in my relationships?* My hope is that you'll become more informed, relational, and God-honoring and that you'll trade any confusion you might have for clarity on your path to finding "the one."

THE COUNTERCULTURAL PATH

1

Lauren F. Winner

IN HER RECENT NOVEL *THE OUTSIDE WORLD*, TOVA MIRVIS DESCRIBES the acquaintanceship, engagement, and marriage of two young New Yorkers, Tzippy and Baruch. I know *acquaintanceship* is an awkward noun, but I use it because no other word will do. What Tzippy and Baruch have is not quite a romance. They don't exactly date, but they don't quite court, either. The match they make is not quite arranged, nor can it be mistaken for the match Monica and Chandler made on *Friends*.

Tzippy and Baruch are orthodox Jews, straddling — as many real-life, nonfictional Christians straddle — two different schools of premarital sociability. There's modern-day romance on one hand, and then there's the traditional way of doing things.

In some corners of the orthodox Jewish world, the traditional way of doing things is called *shidduch* dating (*shidduch* literally means "match"). *Shidduch* dating is not entirely unlike contemporary Christian courtship; when one is of marriageable age, friends, relatives, and other folks in the community begin thinking up suitable mates. If the parents approve and the young man and woman themselves are willing, the couple goes out for a first date, the goal of which is not to flirt or practice coquetry but to get to know one another with the speed and precision of a laser so they can each ascertain whether the other might be an appropriate marriage partner. If things seem promising, there is a second date and a third, and after a fairly short time, a decision is made—either the couple gets engaged, or they call it quits.

Tzippy goes on an unusually long string of *shidduch* dates arranged by friends, relatives, and fellow synagogue-goers before she finally meets Baruch. Her dates are "arranged through an elaborate circuitry, transmitted by connections once, twice, thrice removed." (The dates generally comprise a Diet Coke and conversation in a hotel lobby, lobbies being popular orthodox dating spots because they are so public that something untowardly intimate or sexual couldn't possibly happen.) By her forty-second *shidduch* date, Tzippy

> felt as if she were drowning. . . . It used to sound easy. How hard could it be to determine compatibility? . . . The main objective was to discover if there was potential for marriage. Do you want to live in New York or in Israel? . . . Would you allow a television in your home? Do you go to the movies? The yeses would be tabulated against the nos and a decision would be made as to whether the person sitting across the table was The One.[1]

Date number forty-two is a bust, and Tzippy decides to leave New York for a year to study in Jerusalem. There, she spies the son of her mother's college roommate, a boy she hasn't seen since childhood. Baruch, too, is studying in Israel for a year. Tzippy begins, in very un-orthodox fashion, to follow him around Jerusalem until they finally meet face-to-face. Instantly smitten, they know they can't simply start dating; they must recreate that "elaborate circuitry" *post facto*. So they contact friends and friends of friends who arrange a *shidduch* date, and that date is followed by a whirlwind courtship. Soon enough, Baruch and Tzippy are engaged, and not long after, married.

The Outside World, though set in a community of orthodox Jews, beautifully captures all that is appealing and all that is problematic about dating for a religious person in any religious community in contemporary America. There is something very compelling about the *shidduch* system. As Tzippy muses,

> The rabbis assured them that their way of getting married was so much better than in the outside world. Here, people gave advice about which college to go to . . . even which nursery school to choose. . . . But when it came to marriage—the most important decision of all—you were supposed to rely solely on your feelings.[2]

Shidduch dating offers an attractive alternative to the unrealistic romanticism and palpable sexuality of modern American dating. And yet even for Baruch and Tzippy, a little modern-day romance creeps in. Even in their modest, regimented, almost cloistered world, Tzippy's and Baruch's feelings manage to dictate, or at least shape, their choice. Their eventual courtship can be called *shidduch* dating, but barely. After all, Tzippy pursued Baruch through the streets of Jerusalem. They chose each other.

The novel encapsulates many of the questions Christians are asking when they debate, analyze, and consider dating. What is the place of one's family and community in matchmaking? How can one date in a way that is conducive to chastity? And what about those pesky emotions?

Can they be trusted? Or are we to approach potential mates with cool, clinical reason and a checklist of desirable qualities?

A BRIEF HISTORY OF DATING AND ROMANCE IN AMERICA

That Christians today disagree about the best way to court or date is no surprise. We can see, by considering how dating has evolved in America over the last two hundred years, that dating and courtship are social institutions with histories.[3] Americans living in different centuries and places have thought and behaved differently when it comes to dating, romance, love, and marriage.

In the colonial era, there was no such thing as dating. Marriages were often arranged. People may have hoped to marry someone they liked, but the main purposes of marriage were a little more mundane: You married someone with whom you could rear children; you married someone in a family with whom your family wanted an alliance; you married someone whose inheritance would augment your land holdings; you married someone because you wanted to have licit sex. Eighteenth-century Americans were often quite frank about these less-than-starry-eyed reasons to marry. Founding father George Mason, for example, explained that he remarried after several years of being a widower not because he was in love but because his "bed had grown cold." And many widows pointedly avoided remarrying for equally unromantic reasons: As widows, they controlled their own money, but should they remarry, they would lose control of their property to their husbands. For many women, no romance could outweigh fiscal independence.[4]

By the last third of the nineteenth century, things had begun to change. Marriage was still about economic and procreative concerns, to be sure, but more and more often, people hoped to marry someone they loved, someone they adored. And as expectations for marriage changed, the way people paired off changed, too. Gradually, a system of calling came to replace the betrothals and arranged marriages of the nineteenth century. To be sure, parents and families still played an important part in matchmaking, insofar as parents generally approved their children's mates. Usually, the pool of potential suitors was still implicitly limited to those within the family's social circle. Young men called on young women, first seeking parental approval to visit, and often the couple kept company on the girl's family's front porch or in their parlor.

At the turn of the century, people began dating. A popular—if possibly apocryphal—story from the 1920s illustrates the transition from calling to going out on dates. A young man asked a lady he admired if he might call on her. She consented, and the pair set a time for their meeting. When the man arrived, the lady was wearing a hat, a gesture that conveyed a world of change. The man came expecting to visit in the parlor, but the woman, who would never wear her hat inside her parents' parlor, clearly expected to be taken out—and in the end the young man did take her out, spending a month's salary to meet the expectations of a date.[5]

The transformation in American social life from calling to dating brought with it many subtler shifts. Romance no longer bloomed under the watchful eye of parents, and relationships increasingly developed in public spaces—not front parlors and family rooms but movie parlors and restaurants. Dating also required money because the system of going out on dates—to an ice cream parlor or tea shop—placed social relations squarely in the world of the market.

Money's role in dating meant that the dynamics between men and women shifted. In the old system of calling, women had a tremendous amount of authority. Women arranged their own social lives, deciding when to hold "at-home" days to receive callers. Indeed, in the calling system, women were far from passive dolls on pedestals waiting to receive visitors. Rather, it was the lady who initiated visits. *Fin de siécle* etiquette books make quite clear that it was the "girl's privilege" to "ask a young man to call."[6] (The unquestioned patriarchy of current Christian courtship, then, is actually something of an innovation. This, perhaps, is something that current-day advocates of courtship should bear in mind before appealing to tradition as a means of shoring up a system of gender roles in which men are always to pursue and women are always to wait and be pursued.)

What Do You Think?	Are you surprised by Lauren's assertion that women, until recently, often initiated relationships? How do you react?

As dating replaced calling, gender roles shifted. Because men had the earning power, and dates cost money, roles reversed. Whereas women had been the hostesses on the front porch or in the parlor, men now played host in restaurants and at soda fountains. Indeed, dates became defined as outings that cost money. As historian Beth Bailey sums up,

> Over and over in the national media, women and men, girls and boys, advisers and experts insisted on this definition of dating. Money was central: a date took place when a couple "went out" and spent money. . . . American youth did not consider spending time with a member of the opposite sex the same as dating. . . . [A] date centered around an act of consumption: going out for dinner or a Coke, seeing a movie.[7]

Even the language used to describe romantic connections changed to reflect the changes in dating practices: Whereas an earlier generation spoke of "keeping steady company"—say, on the front porch—new daters talked of "going steady"—*going* out into the world.

In the 1960s, American dating changed again. As people delayed marriage and as the sexual revolution unfolded, relationships became more frankly sexual. Romantic relationships returned to the private sphere—this time not the parental parlor but the bedrooms of the dating couple.

And in the last decade, dating has come under some rather fierce assaults from quite divergent corners. Some American Christian communities have begun to question dating, suggesting that it is too sexual, too emotional, or too individualized, and arguing that serial monogamy while single does little to prepare people for a lifetime of marital fidelity. Dating is seen in some Christian communities as "unbiblical" or "too worldly," and Christian critics have suggested that Christian men and women (or, more often, "guys and girls") hang out in groups, spend time together with their families, and court rather than date.

Ironically, at the same time that some Christians have critiqued dating, many secular folks have abandoned the etiquette and responsibilities of dating and have opted instead for sexual encounters with friends. Skipping the tedious rituals of dating, such as taking someone to the movies or treating her to dinner, they instead just phone a friend and arrange a sexual encounter, neat and simple. This abandonment of dating in favor of "friendship with privileges," as it has come to be called, has taken hold even in the teenage realm. Consider Caity, a fourteen-year-old who recently "hooked up" with a guy she met at the mall. Benoit Denizet-Lewis reported on Caity and her friends in a recent article in *The New York Times*:

I ask Caity if that's it, or if her hookup might lead to something more. "We might date," she tells me. "I don't know. It's just that guys can get so annoying when you start dating them." Adam, a 16-year-old sophomore at the end of the table, breaks in, adding that girls, too, can get really annoying when you start dating them.[8]

Groups such as the Independent Women's Forum have taken out ads in college newspapers calling for students to "Take Back the Date," but these campaigns seem to be having little impact.[9]

We can see, then, that throughout American history, there have been certain trends in the social organization of romance. One trend has been away from the authoritative involvement of parents. Another trend has been out of the home and into the public sphere—though since the sexual revolution, that trend has ironically reversed itself, as dating couples have retreated to the privacy of apartments and houses. We've also seen that as the average marriage age increases, people go on dates with more people over a greater number of years. What are Christians to make of these trends? Are we to critique them, participate in them, or somehow do both selectively?

HOW SCRIPTURE PRESSES US TO ASK QUESTIONS ABOUT LOVE, NOT ABOUT DATING OR COURTSHIP

The book that energized much of the courtship movement was Joshua Harris's *I Kissed Dating Goodbye*. In general, I am not a big fan of courtship. I bristle at the rigidly prescribed gender roles that Harris and many other proponents of courtship take for granted. And I wonder about the idealized parental and community involvement that courtship suggests, for courtship—both in the nineteenth-century American sense and in the twentieth-century *I Kissed Dating Goodbye* sense—requires a robust, stable, institutionally strong community. Tzippy and Baurch, our fictional orthodox Jews, make this plain; their *shidduch* dating would have been both impossible and unintelligible outside the context of a tight-knit, enclosed community. Some Christians in contemporary America do live in such thick communities, but most of us don't. And though many of us desire such communities, basing relationship models on the assumption that all single Christians live in thriving Christian communities is perhaps putting the proverbial cart before the horse. If you are a twenty-six-year-old who has just moved across the country for grad school, the role your community can play in your romantic life will be different from the place of community in the life of the twenty-six-year-old who grew up in a small town, went to the local college, and now works at the local bookstore. By the same token, there is little opportunity for your parents to be intimately involved in your romantic life if you are removed—emotionally, geographically, or spiritually—from them.

It is worth noting that when one actually reads Harris's books—both *I Kissed Dating Goodbye* and its sequel, *Boy Meets Girl*—one finds that convenient caricatures of courtship will not do. For starters, Harris kissed dating good-bye not primarily because he thought dating was an abomination but because he thought he was too young to marry, and he believed one ought not date, court, or otherwise engage the emotions of a potential mate if one had no intention of marrying. When, in *Boy Meets Girl*, he sketched out a system in which men and women who were ready for the altar could meet and fall in love and marry, he termed it "courtship." But he also said that an endless debate over terminology was not salutary. Almost any Christian, even the most devoted dater, could endorse the basic principles he sketched out for courtship: In relationships, "submission to [God's] Word is nonnegotiable"; we should follow the Golden Rule and strive to selflessly do "what's best for the other person"; we should include the larger community, relying on the wisdom, encouragement, and "support of our church"; we should commit to sexual chastity and remember that God is the ultimate "object of our soul's longing."[10]

This interminable parsing of terms — do we date, court, or something else? — is, it seems to me, precisely the sort of debate that Jesus detested when he found it among the Pharisees. The central question is not, "Are we to date, to court, or to enter into arranged marriages?" but, "What is the central command of the Christian life, and how is it to bear on our social relations?" The first half of that question is easy. The central command of the Christian life is the two-pronged love command: to love the Lord our God with all our hearts, minds, and souls and to love our neighbor as ourselves. The task of contemporary Christians is to discern how the love command can shape our friendships, romances, marriages, and communities.

You may have attended a seminar or read a book purporting to lay out "the biblical view of dating." But, in fact, there is no biblical view of dating, for dating is not a biblical category. There was no such thing as dating during biblical times, just as there were no automobiles, no fast-food restaurants, no capitalism, no halter tops, no master's degrees, no scented candles, and no Internet. So Christians who want to think Christianly about dating or fast food can't simply look up *McDonald's* or *date* in a biblical concordance and flip to the relevant verses in Scripture. Rather, we must read Scripture carefully and coherently, looking for the narratives, patterns, and principles that can guide us in making ethical decisions about situations that didn't exist in biblical times, situations that are historically specific to the modern (or post-modern) era.[11]

Consider, by way of example, the Internet. The Bible obviously doesn't have anything specific to say about the Internet. But it does give us general principles that might guide how we are to engage new technologies: We are to steward them, not to make idols out of them; we are not to allow them to wreck Christian rhythms of time; we are to evaluate their merits by asking not whether they make life easier but rather whether they promote human flourishing. We are to somehow engage technology in a way that keeps the love command ever before us.

Similarly, the Bible says nothing per se about dating.[12] But it does have plenty to say about how we shape our social relations. For example, Genesis makes it clear that community, friendship, and marriage are good things. The Creation story tells us that we are rightly intrigued by and drawn to one another. Friendship, romance, hanging out in groups, learning to love the folks in our churches, attending to our families, entering into and sustaining marriages—all of these can be right expressions of the biblical insight that it is not good for man to be alone. Participating in these relationships and communities is part of what it means to be human. And participating in these relationships is part of how the image of God works.

Certainly, there is a wealth of biblical teaching on relationships in general that ought to be applied to any Christian friendship, romance, or dating relationship. We are to show one another mutual respect; we are to love one another with care, compassion, patience, and a willingness to forgive. Christians in relationship with one another must ask themselves, *How do I respect this person, how do I care for him or her, what is courtesy, and what is kindness?* Scripture similarly has teachings about sexuality that will shape how Christians date. Sex is not appropriate before marriage, but sexuality is inescapably in play in human relationships, and we must make choices about stewarding our sexuality.

Christian relationships are to be conceived inside a larger frame, which is the kingdom of God and the body of Christ. Our relationships need to be redemptive and in keeping with God's purposes in the world. As the apostle Paul tells us in Romans 12:2, Christians are often asked to distinguish ourselves from the prevailing patterns of society. As we date, then, our task is to discern how the prevailing patterns of dating are distorted and in conflict with what we understand to be good, wise, and pleasing to God. We are required to have some consciousness, sophistication, and savvy about how to avoid conforming to the world.

This means, of course, that Christians will not take their dating cues principally from the surrounding culture. If Christian dating may look, in some ways, like the dates we read about in chick lit, it will also differ markedly from the dating Bridget Jones does. Christian dating is, in short, countercultural. To say that is not to engage in a flat-footed critique of the secular culture. It is rather to suggest that the Christian story leads us to relate to each other in a way that is distinctively Christian. Christian dating is chaste, communal, and oriented toward marriage. It partakes of Christian love, a cruciform love that should be very different from the love described in the pages of *Maxim* and *Cosmo*.

CHASTITY AND CHRISTIAN DATING

Perhaps the most obvious arena in which Christian dating is distinctive is its commitment to chastity. Chastity is one of those uncomfortable, old-fashioned, exceedingly churchy words, but it is unavoidable when talking about Christian dating. The ethic of sex developed in Scripture, beginning in Genesis and continuing through the Epistles of Paul, makes clear that sex was created for marriage and that all Christians are called to lives of chastity.[13] For unmarried folks, chastity means no sex at all, and for married folks it means sex only with one's spouse. Living chastely before marriage is, to be sure, difficult, in large part because our society delays marriage longer than any previous generation in American history.

It is hardly necessary to note that we live in a sex-saturated society, that popular culture uses sexual images and sexual talk nonstop, and that the messages the secular world gives us about sex are very much at odds with the biblical vision of sexuality. In the idiom of secular society, good sex is frequent, casual, and has no consequences. In the Christian grammar, by contrast, good sex is conditioned by context—good sex, real sex, is sex that happens in marriage. Secular society tells us, simultaneously, that sex is no big deal and that it's the most important thing in the universe. Sex is so banal and meaningless that we can have random, casual sex with our next-door neighbor, yet sex is so hugely significant that we can't possibly live without it. So one challenge single Christians face is sensitizing themselves to and thinking critically about the confusing messages pop culture sends us about sex.

Practicing chastity, especially when one is dating, raises a host of practical questions. If practicing chastity means reserving sex for marriage and safeguarding marital sexuality, then dating Christians rightly want to know what expressions of physical intimacy between an unmarried man and woman might be appropriate and even good. When I began dating Griff, the man to whom I'm now married, we sought the wise input of a married friend we hoped could guide us in our pursuit of chastity. We wanted to know what everyone else who's dating wants to know: How far is too far? Yes, we could be self-critical of that question; we knew the question sought to reduce good biblical teaching about gracious and salutary marital sex to a list of dos and don'ts. But at the end of the day, we still wanted some practical guidance. Our friend, a campus pastor at the University of

Virginia who knew our particular biographies well, sized up the situation and gave us this suggestion: "Don't do anything sexual that you wouldn't be comfortable doing on the steps of the Rotunda," the dome-shaped building that sits at the heart of the university. We took his advice to heart. We even climbed up on the Rotunda's steps one night and kissed to our hearts' content—and then said, "Well, that's it; there's our line. We don't really feel comfortable stripping our clothes off up here in front of the Rotunda." And that became our mantra: on the steps of the Rotunda.

You'll notice that our rule came from a friend, someone within our trusted community. We wanted his input as we established our guidelines because he knew us well, and he was older, married, and wise. Chatting with friends, family, or pastors about such intimate matters can, to be sure, feel embarrassing and awkward. But I have found that involving my community in setting guidelines—about sexuality, about money, about how I spend my time—has actually been a relief. It has removed some of the decision-making weight from my lone shoulders. And it has helped me establish practices, patterns, and behavioral guidelines that make sense for me and my particular relationships—far better, I think, than a one-size-fits-every-Christian rule. And, when your physical relationship is communally protected, you're more likely to maintain a discipline of chastity that's just as holy as prayer or fasting.

But chastity is more than just line drawing. It is more than just gritting your teeth and keeping your zipper zipped. And chastity is more than avoiding any remote opportunity to make sexual mistakes. (It seems a lot of dater-haters want to do away with dating simply because they think dating, or allowing males and females to be alone at all, will lead to sex.) Chastity is not merely about the negative, the refraining from something. It is also positive. And it is active in at least two ways. It is active because it involves a positive safeguarding of marital sexuality, and it is active because it involves orienting one's self toward God in a particular way. There is a lot of Christian talk about the eroticism of modesty and chastity. We in the church, eager to uphold single folks in their pursuit of chastity, often say that modest dress and chaste behavior are actually a lot more alluring than letting it all hang out. This may, of course, be true. But to focus on the allure of modesty is to miss the point of chastity. If one chooses clothes with high necklines and avoids making out but is still fixated on attracting Prince or Princess Charming, one may not be practicing chastity at all. True chastity involves disciplining our sexual desires and turning our focus away from members of the opposite sex toward God alone.

COMMUNITY AND CHRISTIAN DATING

I have suggested that one of the problems with the courtship model is that it presupposes a rich community that is not available to many contemporary American Christians. The popularity of Internet dating emphasizes how atomized many Americans are. Secular sites such as match.com and Christian sites such as Christiancafe.com have filled a void. At one time, communities would have served the role of matchmaker. Parents would have introduced their kids to one another; friends and cousins and even professional matchmakers would have been on the lookout. But today, communities don't exist in the same way. We Americans are a geographically mobile bunch; we move around, and when we do settle in one place, we often barricade ourselves in a gated community. We generally are too busy or too indifferent to check on our neighbors when they are in the hospital, let alone introduce them to potential mates. The Internet has stepped into the matchmaking breach.

| **What Do You Think?** | How have you reacted to the trend of Internet dating? Do you consider it a valid approach to finding "the one," or have you dismissed it entirely? |

Still, to question the precise ways in which courtship involves community is not to suggest that there is no Christian community or that Christian community ought not play a part in dating, romance, and the discernment of a call to marriage. On the contrary, Christian dating can and ought to be communal for several reasons. First, community is a Christian imperative. Christian dating should be communal because all of Christian life is communal. For Christians, both the ethical unit and the unit of discernment is not the individual but the community. Christians are, after all, members of a people, the people of Israel and the people of the church. We are elected as a people and redeemed as a people, and we conduct our ethical and social lives in communal rather than individual terms.

Second, Christian dating is communal because dating points toward marriage and, properly understood, Christian marriage is communal. Our surrounding society tells us that marriage is a private endeavor, that what happens between husband and wife behind closed doors is no one else's concern. But in Christian terms, marriage is not merely for the married; it is also for the church, because marriage hints at and reminds us of the eschatological union between Christ and the church. That sounds like complicated theological abstraction, but it has practical implications for the shape of Christian relationships. We Christians are called to be in relationship with one another, and we are called to be transparent before one another. One particular way married people can do that is by displaying the real work of their marriages—not just the sweet, light parts of marriage but also the hard, embattled parts—to unmarried folks. This is important because it allows unmarried Christians to see what real marriage looks like. And it is important because marriage is a gift God gives the church. Marriage is not designed to benefit only the married couple. Rather, it is designed to tell a story to the entire church, a story about God's own love and fidelity to us.

But what does it actually mean to call Christian dating communal? It does not mean that a Christian man and woman should go only on group dates—in fact, it is vitally important for dating couples to spend lots of time alone. When we talk one-on-one, walk one-on-one, and even sit in coffee shops reading one-on-one, we learn important things about one another. But these tête-à-têtes are just one way we come to know and be known. People are multifaceted, and if some of our facets are revealed in quiet dinners with our beau, other facets show up at large potluck suppers with our friends. So it is important that couples spend time alone, but it is also important that they spend time with their friends and communities—not only hanging out with other single folks but also getting to know married couples and families. The burden rests not just on single Christians to go out and get to know the married people in their church but also on the church to work against the pervasive ethic of demographic segregation—an ethic that seeks to sequester singles in one Sunday school classroom, young married couples in another, senior citizens in a third—by fostering relationships among Christians of all ages and stations. And the burden is on married people to open their homes to their single friends. This doesn't just mean inviting people over for dinner. It means going grocery shopping together, going on vacation together, doing laundry together; it may even mean living together in an intentional community. It means Christians inviting other Christians into their homes and into their lives.

A student in one of my writing workshops, an unmarried Christian woman in her forties, wrote about this in an essay titled, simply, "Relationships":

> I love being a part of families. I don't feel quite whole merely hanging around with other unconnected singles, trying to act as if we have more than one thing in common: which is, specifically, the shared lack of something. . . . It's wonderful coming home to someone's house and hearing, "I'll be right down" yelled out in your general direction. Seating yourself at the kitchen table and picking at the bowl of homemade granola or grabbing a glass of water because you know where the glasses are kept. Greeting all the other family members who meander in—none surprised to find you there at 7 a.m. or noon or 10:30 at night. When your own make-yourself-at-home family is hundreds or thousands of miles away, you just need to borrow a family, find a spot and snuggle in. Finding a spot, for me, has meant everything from making the rounds of soccer practices and piano recitals, to dropping by unexpectedly and knowing there's always a spot at the table, to squatting beside the tub for the bedtime bath routine. It's a matter of celebrating the really big things and also sharing in the daily-ness of life.

Later, my student describes how these relationships, these communities, are part of her relationship with her new beau, David:

I find myself wanting to pull David into all of my important relationships, for several reasons. For one, I just want people I really, really like to know each other. And enjoy each other. But I also want these friends who know me and love me and look out for me to be "in" on the process of saying, "Yes, David brings out a part of you that we love and have always wanted to see more of." I want our relationship to be a celebration of everything that I am and have already shared with others I love, not a somehow secretive and isolated portion of the inner me.

LOVE AND CHRISTIAN DATING

One theme that has emerged in the debate over courtship and dating is the place of emotions—particularly romantic love—in the Christian life. Some champions of dating suggest that emotional intimacy within proper bounds is a fine thing between a dating couple. Courtshippers, on the other hand, seem much more committed to protecting the emotional lives of the unmarried. When skimming Amazon.com's reader reviews for I Kissed Dating Goodbye, one begins to wonder if people are avoiding dating principally because they want to avoid getting hurt. "Are you tired of the pain and anguish after a breakup?" asks one enthusiastic reader. "Do you want to avoid the 'dating and heartbreaking cycle?'"[14] Then try courtship! Similarly, one young man who is betrothed to a young woman for whom he used to babysit put it this way in an article in The New York Times: "I can begin to emotionally connect because it's safe. You're not going to leave in six months and break my heart."[15]

But perhaps avoiding pain should not be our main concern in thinking about dating and courtship. Christians ought to strive to protect one another's hearts as they date, but dating involves risk and vulnerability, and risk and vulnerability often involve heartache. To focus, in any of our relationships, on minimizing pain and risk may be to avoid what love entails. As theologian Diogenes Allen writes in his wonderful (and woefully out-of-print) book *Love*, "It is not just in moments of beauty and warmth that God's love finds its way into us, but also through traumatic experiences of . . . rejection."[16] One who is obsessed with protecting her heart runs the risk of having a heart that becomes unbreakable. Christians should strive not to avoid pain but rather to inhabit a love that is Christian, even cruciform.

Søren Kierkegaard, a nineteenth-century Danish philosopher and theologian, once wrote that God's work in Christ "has changed everything, has changed love as a whole."[17] Just what is this changed love? What is properly ordered love from a Christian perspective? Trying to answer that question would require a book in itself. Let me simply sketch the beginning of a Christian understanding of love, especially as it relates to the question of dating. Christian love, surely, is modeled on God's love for us—a love expressed in creation and a love expressed on the cross. And it is a love that is directed toward an other—or, more precisely, to two others: to our beloved and to the One who made us.

Through romantic love, even romantic love that ends in a painful breakup, we often learn important lessons. By this I don't mean to therapeutically say, "Break-ups are fine as long as you Keep Your Chin Up, Look Inward, and Learn Something About Yourself."[18] Rather, I mean that the exhilarating experience we call infatuation, not to mention the exhilarating experience we call falling in love, can actually teach us something about loving our neighbor. Again, Diogenes Allen expresses it well:

When falling in love, we seem to float on air. The whole world seems wonderful, and we take in stride people who normally irritate us and things that normally frustrate us. . . . A particular person's idiosyncrasies, which normally rub us the wrong way, no longer affect us adversely. For a while, we simply seem to be able to love anyone — to love our neighbor — without any effort at all. These momentary occasions can . . . give us a glimpse of what it would be like to love our neighbor all the time.[19]

In the Christian idiom, love is not merely — or even primarily — an emotion. Indeed, classic Christian wedding vows make clear that our emotions are, if not wholly irrelevant, at least not the principal point of marriage. At a wedding, brides and grooms pledge to love each other until one of them dies, a pledge that makes no sense if love is only a feeling. After all, I have little control over my feelings; I can't promise someone I will have a certain set of feelings about him next week, let alone next year or in fifty years. Marriage vows make sense only if the couple's love is the *agape* love of the New Testament, Christian love, love that is about a choice to serve someone and to be loving toward him regardless of what you happen to feel that morning. (As I type, my husband is making me coffee. I think he is annoyed because I snapped at him last night and haven't yet apologized. He would probably prefer to make tea for himself, but he is making me coffee first because that is, in some small way, what he promised at our wedding to do.)

Love, of course, can become an occasion for sin (and in this instance, I'm not talking mainly about illicit sex). We can, after all, love incorrectly, improperly. When we are "in love" with someone, we often appear to attend to our beloved when in fact we are doing the very opposite. Instead of being attentive, we are acquisitive. We use the other for our own glorification; we bask in the presence of our beloved because we enjoy the image of ourselves that is reflected back. We run the risk of loving the image we have concocted of our beloved rather than loving him for who he really is. In Søren Kierkegaard's words, *"It is important that we do not substitute an imaginary idea of how we think or could wish that this person should be.* The one who does this does not love the person he sees but again something unseen, his own idea or something similar."[20] This is the opposite of Christian love. This opposite is all about me. Even idolizing my beloved — certainly a danger for the newly infatuated — is all about me, though it pretends to be all about the other; it is all about me because it does not take my beloved seriously as a person created and redeemed by God but rather imagines him to be perfect, heroic, sublime, and customized to meet my needs.[21] These distortions of love, from idolizing our beloved to basking in the reflection of ourselves that we see in our beloved, are both deformations of Christian love. They fail, ultimately, to be directed toward the other. Indeed, they barely take account of the other at all.

In sketching a Christian alternative to this distorted love, we would do well to turn to Kierkegaard, who once wrote that in order to love, we must first have a "heart bound to God."[22] In her study of Kierkegaard, ethicist Amy Laura Hall develops several characteristics of what she terms "faithful love." Faithful lovers recognize that the beloved is truly another person and not to be used for the lover's purposes. Put more positively, a lover is called to recognize that his beloved is his equal before God. We love our beloved first as a person who is in a relationship with God. Hall says it this way: "By understanding the ones to whom we related as being first related to God, we come to acknowledge their actual selfhood apart from any image, dream, or plan we have for them." Our intimacy with our beloved, in other words, is based first on their relationship with God and on our relationship with God—long before it is based on our relationship with one another.[23]

For Kierkegaard, Christian love is possible only when we, in Hall's words, "repeatedly . . . turn toward God. . . . If we hope to love, we must fall to our knees before the One who intercedes on our behalf." Only when we ground our love for one another in a recognition of our own sin—and of Christ's saving work—is a properly ordered Christian love possible. In this love, says Hall, we see our beloved as created and redeemed by God, and we recognize that our beloved belongs to God before he belongs to us. In Christian love, "each individual lov[es] God alongside of one another, supporting each other to the extent that each one can" but never forgetting that God is our truest Lover. Because we know that our beloved belongs first to God, we strive to purge our love of possessiveness. Finally, when we love in the context of our debt to a gracious God, we come to see that "love involves bestowal, not investment," so we do not look for a "return" on our love.[24]

This love, of course, is an awesome task. The very awesomeness reminds us that without God's grace, we would be incapable of such a selfless, other-directed love.

One place God bestows the grace to love is in marriage. And so, in seeking to sketch a Christian understanding of romantic love and dating, we turn finally to marriage.

MARRIAGE AND CHRISTIAN DATING

For Christians, dating involves, at least implicitly, the question of marriage. To use a theological term, we can say that Christian dating is generally teleological. *Telos* is the Greek word for end point, destination, or goal, so to say that something is teleological is to say that it is moving toward a certain end point or destination. The *telos* of Christian dating, broadly speaking, is marriage. This is not because Christianity believes that marriage is the highest good, that married people are more spiritual than unmarried people, or that marriage is a guarantee of happiness. Rather, it is precisely because the self-sacrificial love you just read about is such a tall order. If romantic love teaches something about loving our neighbors, marriage is an institution that gives us a very near neighbor. If Christian love requires that we recognize our beloved as another person, truly and wholly distinct from ourselves, then marriage, in which we vow to seek what is best for our beloved, offers us an opportunity to distinguish ourselves from another. In Diogenes Allen's words, "The institution of marriage enables the love a man and a woman feel for each other to achieve its own ends: to love well, always, and faithfully."[25]

Contemporary Christians straddle two competing understandings of marriage: the romantic, "companionate" marriage (or love match) and the notion of marriage as politics, marriage as a love that is enacted and incarnated, regardless of whether it is felt. On the one hand, we affirm some notion of romantic love. We look to our dating relationships, and eventually to our marriages, to bring us happiness and emotional satisfaction. On the other hand, Christian marriage is not premised on a romantic fantasy but on the love of God and on our ability, in the context of God's love, to make radical commitments to another person. Our promise to love in marriage is not a promise to feel some set of emotions toward the other person but to live lovingly toward our spouse, despite the capricious whims of our emotional lives.

Christian ethicist Stanley Hauerwas has provocatively quipped that "you always marry the wrong person." There will always be days when you wake up and think, *What have I done? Who is this person? I don't even like her, let alone love her.* It is the call of Christian marriage to love this wrong person, to love this stranger who is your nearest neighbor, even during those days and weeks and years when you feel sure your marriage was a colossal mistake. (To illustrate the point, let us return briefly to Tzippy and Baruch in *The Outside World.* Tzippy and Baruch do eventually get married, and, ironically, they move away from New York—away from the communities and families who shaped their childhoods and romance and engagement and wedding—to the strange and foreign city of Memphis. And there they find, true to Hauerwas's prophecy, that they have married the wrong person, that they have married strangers. Tzippy begins to itch to go to college. Baruch fantasizes about turning his small kosher restaurant into an empire. They sleep in the same bed every night, but sometimes they feel as if they are sleeping alone—or, at least, they wish they were. Ultimately, they go home to New York to celebrate Passover and somehow find their way to each other again; this is how the novel ends, but of course for Tzippy and Baruch it is really only the beginning. They will fall away from each other over and over again, and they will come back to each other each time. They will change, and they will get stuck in ruts, and somehow in all of this, they will make a marriage.)

To say that Christian dating moves toward marriage needs to be qualified. I do not mean that every Christian dating relationship ought to end in marriage, nor do I mean that a dating relationship that does not end in marriage is a failure. Rather, I mean that marriage is the context of Christian dating; one question that Christian men and women need to ask themselves as they embark on dating relationships is, *Am I ready for marriage? Do I think this relationship is heading toward marriage?* If, for example, twenty-nine-year-old Kelli has been dating Matthew for eight months and realizes that for whatever reason she cannot or will not marry him, she probably needs to end the relationship.

The particular ways the teleology of marriage plays out, however, may differ with circumstance or life stage. Two examples should make this clear. First, let us consider dating in high school. I'll explore a high school dating scenario in more detail later in this essay. For now, suffice it to say that in today's society, people are unlikely to marry their high school sweethearts. But it does not follow from that sociological observation that high school dating is forbidden. Rather, the context of marriage—and the improbability that two high schoolers will marry one another—should shape the dating experience. For high schoolers, the improbability of marriage suggests that dating relationships should abide by certain constraints and boundaries. At this stage in life, it's good to see dating as a school, as an opportunity to learn to care about another person. Because marriage is probably a very distant *telos*, high schoolers ought to involve parents and pastors and communities who can create a social context in which the teens won't awaken either emotional or physical desires that must go unfulfilled. In practical terms, this might mean submitting to curfews. It might mean going on a few old-fashioned double dates. It might mean bucking current trends, such as spending late-night hours on the phone or in IM sessions that can lead to a romantic, uninhibited intimacy for which teenagers may not be ready.

At the other end of the life-stage spectrum, let's consider senior citizens. Imagine a Christian widow and widower in their seventies. Suppose that when their spouses were living, the two couples held season tickets to the local symphony and went out to dinner as a foursome once a month. Imagine, further, that neither the widow nor widower is interested in remarrying. But they are interested in companionship. It would be hard to argue that this couple ought not be able to date—if dating for them means regular companionship, even accompanied by certain special, companionable, emotional intimacies.

Sometimes, of course, Christians find themselves obsessed with marriage. Many juniors and seniors on Christian college campuses, for example, will tell you they feel pressure to have "a ring by spring"—if they're not engaged by the time they graduate, they'll feel that they've failed. In light of this pressure and in light of the contemporary church's all but making an idol out of nuclear families, we can't just say, "Marriage is the goal of Christian dating" and leave it at that. For though marriage may be the *telos* of Christian dating, it is not the goal of Christian living.

Christians must remember that marriage is not a better, more desirable, or more godly state than singleness. In fact, the apostle Paul and the majority of church fathers from Augustine through the reformers looked askance at marriage. They thought it was permissible, but they never held it up as the best example of Christian living. They saw marriage as one state in which people can know and love the Lord, but they never suggested it was the better or only state in which one can live a full life or become a devoted follower of Jesus. In fact, as theologian David Matzko McCarthy has pointed out, Paul's ideal was singleness. Many Christians today aspire to marry, but, says McCarthy, "In 1 Corinthians 7, singleness is the goal. Singleness, for Paul, is an elevation of our natures that depends upon life within the family of God. Singleness is a sign . . . of the riches of the common life." Christians today tend to look down on singleness. But according to McCarthy, "Paul, on the other hand, assumes that marriage ought to look as much like singleness as possible."[26]

| **What Do You Think?** | How do you react to Lauren's assertions about singleness as an ideal state? |

BRASS TACKS: WHAT DOES ALL THIS MEAN FOR MY SATURDAY-NIGHT PLANS?

So what does this mean for how single Christians spend their weekends? The contributors to this anthology have been asked to get down to brass tacks by way of a few specific, if hypothetical, cases—in other words, how do the principles I've outlined apply to real scenarios?

First, a warning: We have to be careful when addressing schematic, hypothetical scenarios because although they give us some information, they might not give us the crucial information—the nuances of community and culture, for example. By taking on these scenarios, I am decidedly not trying to suggest some formula that can be applied across the board. The data supplied in these scenarios—the ages and geographical and familial context of the parties involved—are pertinent, but they are not sufficient. The best dating advice will emerge not from the application of abstractions found in an essay like this one but rather in the context of a community of people who know and love the individuals concerned and can address them not as hypotheses but as particular people.

With that qualification, let me share a few thoughts about our hypothetical single Christians. In the first scenario, we meet two Christian high schoolers, Jenny and David, whose friends tell them they'd make a cute couple. Should they date?

Presbyterian pastor Timothy Keller has made a distinction about dating that pertains to age and life stage: When people are young, they often go on dates because they want to go to a particular event (for instance, a prom, a movie, or a poetry slam) and they'd like some company; as people get older, dating becomes more and more about finding events that can provide an excuse for getting together with a particular person.[27] This is a useful watchword for teenagers and parents thinking and praying about teen dating.

The clear question here is Jenny and David's relative youth. Teen dating needs to be shaped so sixteen-year-olds do not totally give themselves to each other. The point is not for teens to completely swear off dating but rather to steward and shepherd their relationship so that they learn good things but don't awaken emotional and physical desires that can't be fulfilled for years to come. High school dating should proceed in certain social, physical, and emotional parameters. What teens should not do, in other words, is go to the prom, dance forehead to forehead, think it's the most important night of their lives, decide they need to cap the evening by losing their virginity, and then feel disoriented and confused for the next umpteen years. Equally important, dating teens should not develop unmanageable emotional attachments to one another. This is where parents, pastors, and communities come in. Their job is to help high schoolers temper the throes of their love.

Jenny and David's youth pastor will want them to enjoy all that is good and fun and wonderful about infatuation and high school romance, but he or she will want to guide them so they don't do stupid things, such as have sex or become overly absorbed with each other. Puppy love, of course, is irrational, so it's crucial that everyone in teenagers' lives help keep things in perspective. Teenagers' relatives and adult friends can offer the guidance that will prevent teen relationships from accelerating in a sexually or emotionally warped way.

One very practical question about teen dating is the place of technology in teens' social lives. Cell phones and the Internet have had a dramatic impact on teen romance in the last decade. At its most extreme, technology encourages a frank indulgence in sexuality, often unmoored not only from marriage but also from the context of any sort of ongoing romantic relationship. Popular websites encourage teens to select partners for casual sexual hookups. As a cofounder of one of these websites explains,

> You'll never see the word "dating" on our site, because that's much too serious for our demographic. . . . There are obviously relationships that come from the site, but mostly I think it's a lot of hanging out and hooking up. This demographic doesn't want to appear like they're needy and looking for a relationship.[28]

But even teens who haven't wandered on to such sites are affected by technology. High schoolers often sit up late into the night at their computers IM-ing one another. As Benoit Denizet-Lewis has observed, teen cell phone use means that the girl who's interested in dating your son doesn't have to call him at home; she can track him down on his mobile. When I was in high school way back in the early 1990s, my mother refused to let me have a phone in my room. I was angry for months. I thought her desire to monitor my phone talking by keeping me in the den was invasive and unreasonable. Now, predictably enough, it strikes me as wise.

In our second hypothetical scenario, Steve and Rachel, college students at a secular school, "are very attracted to each other." Neither of their families is Christian; Steve has been a Christian for a few years, and

Rachel is a brand-new Christian. Steve and Rachel's conversion stories are salient because they tell us something about their families and their communities. We can presume that Steve and Rachel's primary — perhaps only — Christian community is on campus. Steve and Rachel therefore cannot rely on their parents or siblings as their primary authorities in discerning how to proceed.

The key for Steve and Rachel, then, is to pursue involvement in the church — here I mean the church universal, but I also mean an actual church near their college. Campus ministry is, to be sure, utterly transformative in the lives of many students. But if students never venture from their campus parachurch to an actual church, they will not have many opportunities to forge relationships with older, mature Christians. (One campus pastor, after all, cannot adopt hundreds of college students into his or her life and home.) So I would advise Steve and Rachel to connect with a church and to invite some older, married folks into their lives, both separately and as a couple.

I would hope the older people in Steve's and Rachel's lives would help them think about how they can protect each other emotionally and physically and whether or not they should move toward marriage. As with the high schoolers in the previous example, we don't want Steve and Rachel to go to emotional or sexual places they shouldn't go. A concrete example: If Steve and Rachel, as they process their feelings with their community, do discern a movement toward a deeper, lifelong relationship, then they can have some conversations about marriage, both by themselves and with their friends and mentors. But college sophomores who've been dating for seven weeks probably shouldn't lie on the quad with their toes up in the air staring at the stars and talking about marriage. It's really fun and intense to do that — I had those conversations with about five different guys before I finally got engaged and married — but that doesn't mean it's wise. The conversations I had in college on the quad were indulgent and foolish. When I lay on the quad with Beau X and insisted that our future triplets would be named Flopsy, Mopsy, and Cottontail, I was training myself to treat people as abstractions. I knew this triplet fantasy wasn't going to happen, but I lived in my fantasy world anyway.

One hopes that Steve and Rachel, through church and Christian community, will have wisdom and guidance. Through the church, they can develop relationships with both married and single Christians. Steve and Rachel should hang out with twenty-eight-year-olds who can model responsible dating for them, and they should also be included in the lives of married Christians who can show them what real marriage looks like so that when they are trying to discern their own marital course, they can draw a pattern from the gospel, not from Hollywood.

Our final hypothetical scenario involves Denise, a thirty-year-old professional who lives in a big city across the country from her parents. Despite being active in her church and busy with friends and activities, Denise has not had any real experience with romantic relationships, though she wants to get married and have children. What is she to do?

It is worth noting that though the first two hypothetical examples involved a male and a female, in our final scenario, we have only Denise—a woman who veers slightly toward the stereotype of the busy career gal who fears she might have missed her opportunity to have kids. There is, of course, another almost-stereotype; I'll call him Lothario. Lothario lives, coincidentally, in the same big city as Denise. He grew up in a solidly Christian family, was president of a Christian campus organization during his days at Big State University, and has now been working in finance for seven years. He's a popular guy and has dated lots of women, though few for longer than four months. He claims he very much wants to meet a nice Christian woman, settle down, and raise a family, but he just can't seem to commit. How do we advise him? How do we walk alongside him so he can uncover the source of his fears of intimacy and losing independence? Lothario's friends need to help him think about what it is that makes him balk when he gets past the four-month mark in a relationship.

But back to Denise. Of all our hypothetical scenarios, this is perhaps the hardest to address without more specifics. We know that Denise is not an isolated social unit; she is deeply connected to her church. This ought not be taken for granted—many Christian singles who pray every day and love the Lord with all their hearts have drifted away from the church for seasons ranging from six months to years, often because they feel marginalized in churches full of cooing couples and nuclear families.[29] If Denise had drifted, the first step—well before thinking about her dance card—would be to talk and pray with her about the doctrine of the church.

But Denise already understands the importance of church. So, if I knew Denise, I would seek foremost to be a good friend to her. I'd invite her to soirees and gallery openings and potluck lunches after church. I'd keep my eyes peeled for the perfect match for Denise, and I'd invite them both to a dinner party. In fact, I do know several women like Denise, and this is precisely what I try to do.

Here the church must walk a balance beam that can sometimes be tricky to navigate. It is our task, as the church, to help people marry well (and, once married, to stay married). But we must also be self-critical about the extent to which we hold marriage up as the only Christian option. If I invited Denise to a dinner party, I would try to include a few unmarried men whom I think she might like, but I also would make sure to have an odd number of chairs and guests. Denise, it seems, has not discerned a lifelong call to singleness—her deep desire to marry and have children appears to come from God. But the church must remember that some people are called to singleness—for a lifetime or for a stretch of years or decades—and we don't do Denise any service by ignoring the possibility of that call on her life.

What emerges, I hope, from my attempts to address these three hypothetical scenarios is not so much a formula that can be applied across the board but principles and themes that mark Christian relationships as distinctive. Christian daters are not called first and foremost to protect their own emotional lives nor to track down the "right" marriage partner but to be, in N. T. Wright's phrase, cross-bearers and kingdom-proclaimers. In all our relationships, we should strive to be known as people who stand out from the crowd. We must always try to remember that we are salt, that we must do things in ways that are different and peculiar, ways that might prompt people to ask us questions. ("You and Griff really aren't sleeping together?" one of my non-Christian friends asked me shortly after I got engaged, and it was as good an opening as any to share the gospel.) As Christians, we must form all our social relations in the shape of the cross.

CODA: THE VIEW FROM MY DINNER TABLE

Last night my friend Jimmy came over for dinner. My husband and I adore Jimmy, and we like to think that we are good friends to him. Over pizza, he told me that he'd kissed his girlfriend—this after several months of nonkissing, a pretty remarkable feat for a twenty-nine-year-old ex–punk rocker who's been around the block a few times. And he's having a few doubts: Is this relationship really what he wants? Now that he's kissed his girlfriend, does he need to be thinking seriously about marriage? How will he know if she's "the one"? Or does that matter? "Maybe I could just walk into church and line up all the unmarried women and close my eyes and pick one, since the only real scriptural requirement is that you marry another Christian," Jimmy said.

Then he sipped his water, munched his pizza, and continued: "I feel like there are these two visions, these two worldviews. In one worldview, romance is everything, and marriage is about romantic love, and because marriage is supposed to be forever and lifelong, it is vitally important that you marry the right person. In which case, maybe I shouldn't marry Jasmine because I'm just not sure." Sip, munch. "But then there is this totally different perspective, and that perspective says that marriage is about sanctification, that it is about learning to love someone you may not always dig very much. In which case, I should definitely marry Jasmine because she's basically a great gal, she has a strong faith, we totally get along, and she'll be a good mom. So which is it?"

Which indeed?

Jimmy is right about a lot. There are, broadly, two ways of thinking about marriage, and the way we think about marriage does shape how we think about dating.

We are still finding our way in the middle of a dramatic historical change from marriages that were primarily about familial, social, and economic concerns to marriages that are much more about happiness, emotional fulfillment, and companionship. Of course, there was love before the twentieth century (pick up a Shakespearean play if you think romantic feelings are a newfangled, modern invention). And, of course, contemporary marriage is not all about self-fulfillment; plenty of Americans, Christian or not, make daily sacrifices for the good of their spouses and the good of their marriages. But, still, we are in the middle of a social transformation, and it is perplexing.

For most Christians, the answer to Jimmy's question lies somewhere in the middle. We will date people. We will fall in love. We will make some mistakes. We will get hurt. We will do things that are hurtful. We will spend lots of money going out to eat, and later after we break up with that person, we will think about the Ferragamo pumps we could have bought if only we hadn't wasted our money on all those dinner dates. We will learn a ton about ourselves and how to be in the world, and sometimes we will cry, and sometimes we will feel happier than we ever thought possible. We will think about marriage and wonder exactly what the purpose of marriage is and how we are supposed to know. We will listen to Patsy Cline croon about heartbreak and think she wrote the lyrics just for us. Sometimes we will pick up one of those thick, shiny bridal magazines and get swept up in the fantasy. And one night we will post a profile on Christiancafe.com because you just never know. We will date, and we will romance, and we will try to do those things as Christians, in ways that turn simple romance into gospel living.

THE COUNTERCULTURAL PATH: AN OVERVIEW

Definition

Countercultural dating maintains that the real issue is not to determine a correct dating method but instead to live entire lives—including dating relationships—in obedience and devotion to Christ. Countercultural dating is chaste, it is communal, and it is oriented toward marriage and around Christian love.

Distinctives

- When considering how and when to date, the most important thing to remember is that Christians are called to love first God and then their neighbor. All dating (and every relationship, in fact) should center around that command.

- Christians are called to avoid conforming to the world. Sensitizing themselves to contemporary trends will help them avoid turning the focus of dating away from Christ and to themselves.

- While dating should be oriented toward marriage, breaking up or even dating for the sake of dating isn't necessarily improper. All things considered (especially age), dating implies marriage but doesn't necessarily end in marriage.

- A person's Christian community can and should play a significant role in deciding whom to date and eventually marry.

- Although chastity is an unavoidable call in Christian relationships, it is more than line drawing; instead, it should turn a person from self-centeredness to Christ-centeredness. Kissing can be an appropriate way of expressing sexuality without being sexually immoral.

Key Verses

- Mark 10:29-31

- John 7:7; Romans 12:2; 1 Peter 2:11;
  1 John 2:15 (countercultural)

- Hebrews 13:4

Lauren, however, is quick to point out that one must read Scripture not as a collection of key verses that can be isolated from one another but as a large, beautiful coherent story that reveals truth as much through the whole as through the component parts.

Key Benefits

- Dating can be a godly way to not only meet the love of your life but also learn to love as Christ loves—which includes being hurt, a common symptom of love.

- Dating builds character and can help you make smart decisions about your future mate as you learn to balance romantic love and practical love.

- It's fun! Dating, no matter your age, is an enjoyable way to spend time with another person.

- When you date and even are infatuated, you are able to distinguish a unique love that can be selfless; it can give you a glimpse of what it would be like to love your neighbor all the time.

Potential Problems

- There's a thin line between having fun and getting to know each other and diving too deeply into premature physical or emotional intimacy. Walking that line can be a difficult exercise.

- Depending on your age, stage in life, or call by God, dating may not be appropriate for you.

- In the flurry of falling in love, you could lose the ability to make good decisions or lose sight of your goals. Whether it be through family, church, or godly friends, be sure you allow your community to play a role in your relationships to keep you accountable and available to Christ's body.

THE COURTSHIP PATH

2

Douglas Wilson

IN SHAKESPEARE'S *Much Ado About Nothing*, BENEDICT FAMOUSLY declares, "The world must be peopled!"[1] Not only is this very true, but so far, it has managed to be peopled without much help from me. My three kids and nine grandchildren are just a few drops in the great river of billions, so I don't want to offer this contribution on life between the sexes as the only method that works. In one sense, men and women have been getting together just fine. The job is getting done somehow.

At the same time, we Christians recognize that we live in a fallen world, and the sins that men and women commit are often against each other. This is particularly the case in our American culture, which has in recent decades departed dramatically from biblical standards on such issues as premarital sex, marriage, reproduction, children, education, and more. So the best thing we can do when trying to understand and live out godly dating is to attempt to interpret Scriptures the best we can, regardless of what our culture does.

PRINCIPLES AND METHODS

This book is designed to set different Christian approaches alongside one another and then invite the reader to think through the issues with an open mind and open Bible. In that spirit, I want to begin by noting the important—and to my mind, crucial—distinction between principles and methods. Methods are particular, specific, and necessary. No one can ever do anything without selecting a method for doing it. But at the same time, I don't believe that all methods are created equal. Given a range of choices, we should seek out the method that best suits our circumstances. A central part of doing this is by first understanding the principles involved. Blind allegiance to the method can prevent us from dealing with circumstances in which commitment to the principle would require a different method.

So it's good to recognize that fierce commitment to "a party" doesn't ensure that all wisdom is limited to your side and that all folly is to be found in those "other groups." Put bluntly, I know there are families who are adamantly committed to courtship but who are nevertheless foolish in how they handle themselves. Since I wrote *Her Hand in Marriage*, I have heard more than one courtship horror story. And more than once, I have consequently said that the courtship model means that we have six idiots involved instead of two. In the same way, for any couple who came together in a gracious and wise way by means of (sharp intake of breath) dating, my hat is off to them. I'm mentioning this to recognize on paper that the world is a complex place, but nonetheless, I do believe that the courtship model addresses most successfully the problems that are likely to arise.

WHAT THE COURTSHIP MODEL IS

All this said, we need a working definition of the courtship model. After we have allowed for differences in culture, method, timelines, and so forth, what is the essence of courtship?

As I understand it, courtship is the active, involved authority of the young woman's father in the formation of her romantic attachments leading to marriage. Strictly speaking, we should perhaps say that it's the authority of the head of the household, which is ideally the father (for the sake of this book, we'll use the word *father* to represent whomever the head of the household may be). Because of the widespread fragmentation of the family, many single moms have to work through these issues. In addition, it should go without saying that in a godly marriage, a father will not exercise his authority without depending heavily on the wisdom of his wife.

THE ROLE OF THE FATHER

That said, a father's authority over his daughter in this area is simply a subset of his authority in the family generally. This means that the courtship model is not an egalitarian one. The Bible teaches that under ordinary circumstances, the head of the house is the father and husband. The biblical data supporting this is extensive; here's just one situational example:

> If a woman makes a vow to the LORD, and binds herself by some agreement while in her father's house in her youth, and her father hears her vow and the agreement by which she has bound herself, and her father holds his peace, then all her vows shall stand, and every agreement with which she has bound herself shall stand. But if her father overrules her on the day that he hears, then none of her vows nor her agreements by which she has bound herself shall stand; and the

LORD will release her, because her father overruled her.
(Numbers 30:3-5)[2]

The original context for this passage dealt with financial pledges that were made to the tabernacle. If a wife or daughter made a financial commitment to support the tabernacle, that vow stood if the head of the house ratified it. He could ratify it by saying nothing, or he could ratify it through overt approval. This would also extend to vows made to God of a nonfinancial nature. If, however, the father negated a vow made by his daughter, she was not guilty of having broken her word.

We may apply this to courtship by means of a *fortiori* argument—a "how much more" argument. If a father has the authority to set aside a financial commitment to the God of Israel made by his daughter, how much more does he have the authority to set aside a commitment to go out for coffee that she made to Billy Smith down the street? In other words, if a father has authority in his daughter's life, then surely that authority extends into this important area. It is hard to argue that a father has authority over whether his daughter has car insurance, whether she may get her ears pierced, and so forth but does not have authority if love or sexual temptation is involved.

This is not to argue that the Bible regards women—wives or daughters—as having less than human dignity. The Scriptures also lay out a number of situations where a woman can be independent of both a father and a husband. It would be odd to argue that a forty-year-old widow needs to return to her father's house until she marries again (see Leviticus 22:13). We read in the book of Acts that Lydia was the head of her own household (see 16:13-15). In the book of Ruth, Ruth essentially asked Boaz to marry her without a blessing from any father in sight (instead, she had her mother-in-law's blessing, the mother of Ruth's deceased first husband). And Paul explained that a widow could marry any man she wished, so long as he was a Christian (see 1 Corinthians 7:39). But this goes back to our earlier discussion about principles and methods—these odd situations are not where we are to go to develop our views about what we should ordinarily do.

In the everyday biblical circumstance, sons leave and daughters are given. This pattern was established at the dawn of history: "Therefore a man shall leave his father and mother and be joined to his wife, and they shall become one flesh" (Genesis 2:24). Jesus argued that "from the beginning," this was an important principle (Mark 10:6).

The language of daughters being given in marriage is common in the Bible, just as it is still present in our wedding ceremonies: "Who gives this woman to marry this man?" Of course, given the climate of the times, we should not be surprised when hard-core feminists leave this part out of their marriage ceremonies. Just as they may not take their husband's name (in order to keep their father's name!), so they may not want to be given in marriage. But even in this so-called liberated time, most would think it was more than a little weird to have the groom walk down the aisle and be given away by his mom. This pattern of sons leaving and daughters being given is embedded in us deeply.

Another thought: When a young woman was guilty of sexual fraud in Scripture (representing herself as a virgin when she was not), the result was an execution in front of her father's house. We read about this in Deuteronomy:

> But if the thing is true, and evidences of virginity are
> not found for the young woman, then they shall bring
> out the young woman to the door of her father's house,

> and the men of her city shall stone her to death with
> stones, because she has done a disgraceful thing in
> Israel, to play the harlot in her father's house. So you
> shall put away the evil from among you. (22:20-21)

The execution happened *there* because her father was her God-appointed chaperone. With this point made, I would like to make several qualifications. First, it is crucial to note that this was not an execution for fornication but rather for lying about fornication in the context of a marriage covenant. Second, I am not arguing that this law ought to be reestablished today, unvarnished and whole. Remember the point made earlier about principles and methods. The same Old Testament law that required stoning to death for lying about fornication also required a parapet around the roof of an Israelite's house. This was necessary because they spent a lot of time up there, and the requirement was comparable to our requirements for railings on second-story decks, fences around swimming pools, and covers over wells. Such modern examples fulfill the biblical principle even if the method looks entirely different. A metal covering for a well looks nothing like an ancient Israelite parapet, but we can see the same principle.

That sexual immorality was not a capital crime in ancient Israel can be seen from the following passage in Exodus:

> If a man entices a virgin who is not betrothed, and lies
> with her, he shall surely pay the bride-price for her to
> be his wife. If her father utterly refuses to give her to
> him, he shall pay money according to the bride-price
> of virgins. (22:16-17)

This passage brings us back to the point of our discussion, reinforces the principle of fatherly authority, and at the same time gives us a striking example of the exercise of that authority. In this passage, the father is not saying no to a young man who has expressed honorable interest in his daughter. He is saying no to someone who has already defrauded his daughter, someone who has already seduced her. In other words, this is not casually expressed romantic interest. It is romantic interest that has already been consummated.

Because the young man had defrauded the daughter, her father was in a position to force a marriage if he so desired. He might be able to see that the young man was a decent sort overall and that he could be a good husband for his daughter. But he might also see that the seducer was just a plain old toad, and so he would say no.

In all this, we see that the Scriptures assume that fathers have a practical, applied authority in how and to whom their daughters are given. I am also assuming that the father, if he is wise, will make this decision in close consultation with his wife. A wise woman is the crown of her husband. Basically, the central point I want to argue here is that the daughter is not left alone to fend for herself. Her father watches out for her until the time when her husband will take the responsibility to take care of her.

And now a caution: Sometimes parents can enjoy a vicarious thrill in seeing a relationship come together, even if that relationship is not wise. Just as a father can really want his son to play football so he can relive some of his own "glory days," so a mother can want her daughter to experience the thrill of the prom or the excitement of a new relationship. And no one disputes that such things are fun—if they were not fun, people wouldn't do them. The question is whether they're wise. Ironically, this kind of prodding is more likely if the kids are younger—in other words, the parents are encouraging nothing more than a pleasant evening at the prom. If the kids are older, it is more likely that the relationship could turn serious, and it dawns on the parents that they are betting with real money, not with red and blue chips.

Another parental temptation for the courtship and betrothal models exists when the parents of two families are the closest of friends. One family has a boy and the other a girl—each two years old. It is easy for these parents who get along famously to assume that their little children are "right" for each other. And because they have come to believe in parental authority in such matters, they start assuming with one another that the kids will grow up and get married. The problem here is not that the parents don't have such authority. The problem is that in a fallen world, genuine authority can be foolishly exercised or abused. The fact that someone has the authority to do something does not necessarily make it a wise decision. A father has the authority to stop at the boat dealer on his way home from work and empty out his family's savings account on a hot new ski boat, but that doesn't make it a good idea.

In addition, many parents make the mistake of neglecting their children over the course of many years and then, just as their daughter comes to the age when young men begin coming around, her father suddenly develops very strong and rigid views on how the young man has to "get through him first." In terms of authority on paper, this is quite true and is right at the center of the courtship model. A young suitor should approach a young woman's father. But if the father in this situation has been abdicating for years, he cannot suddenly conjure up a moral authority. When counseling fathers in this kind of situation, I have explained to them that whether they have the right to sign a check in their checkbook and whether they have any money in the account are two entirely separate questions. A father might say that he should be able to tell this suitor no. This is right—he should be able to. But he should have thought of that fifteen years earlier when he was busy building fundamental distrust in his daughter.

When parents abuse authority in this way, what should the young couple do? In our church, we have created a means by which the couple can appeal their situation to the elders of the church. No human authority is absolute, and this includes the authority of the parents in courtship. If a father gave permission for the marriage and then a week before the wedding suddenly reneged for no reason, the couple should be able to appeal somewhere. They should not be left in the awkward position of either obeying a tyrannical decision or deciding to disregard it on their own authority. Almost all the tangled situations of this nature that I have seen have been helped by this kind of external involvement—or could have been helped.

Of course there are times when the suitor is so unsuitable that the father must withhold his blessing regardless of his poor performance in the past. Let's say the suitor is the treasurer for the crack cocaine fund of a local gang. The father should confess his sins of neglect, first to God and then to his daughter, and then refuse to give his blessing. But if, in spite of his neglect, the father wants to say no to a young Christian man who is interested in his daughter just to exercise a little authority for once, he is probably refusing a man who will treat his daughter better than *he* ever did. He should think about this with some humility of mind, though it's probably realistic to assume he won't. If that happens, the couple should return to their church and seek help there.

What Do You Think? How involved is your father in your life? How can you apply what Douglas has said so far to your current relationships with your family and others?

A note about the role of friends: Friends should be there to reinforce the patterns established in a godly family and church. Friends are not to be the source of autonomous wisdom—rather, friends are to function in the context of biblical community. When that community is healthy, the role of friends can provide an important contribution. But friends should not be considered an alternative to family authority. In short, friends should help each other honor their parents and respect the wisdom from those who are older and wiser.

One last comment about this is necessary. In this politically correct day, I could get in deep trouble for saying some of the things I have been saying. I would just like to assert now that the need for men to protect women is inescapable, and everyone in some way acknowledges it. The modern world wants a woman to be protected from sexual harassment, for example. I am arguing for the old-fashioned method of having that protection provided in a much more personal way by fathers, brothers, husbands, and sons. A Christian father, therefore, has the duty to live for his wife and daughters in such a sacrificial and Christlike way that they see that he always has their best interests at heart. And having their best interests at heart means that he has a biblical responsibility to look sideways and squinty-eyed at any suitor that comes around.

SCENARIOS

As we consider the particular scenarios, there is an important consideration we should keep in mind, and that is that every real-life situation has a host of variables. As we sketch these settings, we should be careful to assume average conditions in all things that are not mentioned.

Consider the case of Jenny and David—you know their situation. According to the courtship model, what should they do, if anything?

In my opinion, Jenny and David, no matter how cute they would be together, have no reason to enter into a relationship. As high school juniors, they are sixteen or seventeen years old. They have about seven years to go (on average) before they will be in a position to marry. So that means for the next seven years, provided they stay together, they will struggle with strong sexual temptation, and one of two things will happen. Either they will give in to that pressure, or they will not (mind-blowing stuff, I know). If the former happens, they will have gotten into sexual sin, which we know the Bible prohibits (see 1 Thessalonians 4:3-5). If they keep themselves away from that involvement despite the inevitable pressure, they will be simultaneously exciting and frustrating a God-given desire. This kind of thing done over an extended period of time can lead to serious dislocations in a relationship. Like Tantalus in Hades, they are constantly in close proximity to something desirable that they cannot touch.

Of course, if either—or both—of them say, "Oh, we have spent years together. Staying sexually pure is easy-peasy. Not a moment's trouble," this is either a case of what theologians call lying, or it represents a profound reason why they ought not continue to be in a relationship with one another, as those who pursue marriage should find each other sexually attractive.

Related to this, neither of them has grown up yet, and neither is ready to step into adult responsibilities. If I were David's father, I would take him out to lunch and suggest that after school the next day, he should head down to the car dealer and buy himself a new Lexus. He would stare at me wide-eyed and stammer, "But my paper route won't cover that!" "Ah," I would say. "That is a problem. But you would look cute together." He's not ready for a relationship as much as he's not ready for a Lexus.

None of this is to say it is a sin to marry at a younger age. There are various situations in which David and Jenny could marry young with the blessing of Jenny's father or whomever the head of the household is. The wisdom of this would depend on their relative maturity, David's prospects for providing for a family, and so on.

Now on to Steve and Rachel. According to the courtship model, what should they do?

This scenario presents an interesting variation on the first. There are two significant differences: (1) the couple is in college and therefore closer to the age when they can responsibly marry, and (2) neither has a Christian family to turn to. Let's assume that they are a year or so from graduation. If they came to me for counsel in this situation, I would ask about the condition of their respective families. The fact that parents are not Christians does not mean that Christian kids can dismiss their legitimate parental authority. The Ten Commandments say that we are to honor our father and mother (see Exodus 20:12), and it doesn't specify spiritual orientations. Paul reinforces this when he says this is the first commandment with a promise (see Ephesians 6:2-3). If Rachel has an intact family, I would encourage Steve to approach Rachel's father and ask his permission to get to know his daughter better. He is basically asking for permission to single Rachel out. He should also ask for any parameters that her father would place on the relationship. Provided those parameters do not involve compromising his Christian convictions—"Stop going to church. I hate Jesus freaks."—Steve should do everything he can to honor them.

But suppose that the unbelief in Rachel's family has taken her parents to the extreme. Rachel's dad is a bum she hasn't seen in fifteen years, and her mom directs lesbian workshops for several terrorist organizations. Now what? I would urge Steve and Rachel to seek out an older couple in the church to provide them with some accountability in their relationship. This is not intended to replace the role of parents but to enable them to get a modicum of outside wisdom in what will no doubt be a difficult situation.

Finally we have Denise, the thirty-year-old business professional who is inexperienced with romantic relationships. What should she do?

This is one of the more difficult kinds of situations because it is the problem of a nonrelationship. It reflects upon some broader cultural movements that have resulted in the trend of delaying relationships. And this means that I would not have advice for Denise so much as I would for America. These cultural trends include, but are not limited to, pressure on young women to establish financial independence in a way that runs counter to their desires; widespread immorality, which makes it easier for young men to remain irresponsible and uncommitted; and widespread social distaste for women who are "looking for husbands."

My advice to Denise would be to look for a husband without chasing one. If her peer group lacks a male presence, I would encourage her to move to a place where there are such young men. I would encourage her to do this as close as possible to a place where she can be connected to her family. If she wants to be married (and generally speaking, she should), then she should prepare for marriage. This may mean abandoning the fast-track corporate ladder (if marriage is important to her, risking her career for a change of address is not an unreasonable compromise). Also, preparing for marriage may mean paying close attention to the way she dresses. Immodest and attractive is easy. Modest and repulsive is easy, too. But modest and attractive is an art form.

But this just explains what she should not do. What should she do? In short, she should begin praying specifically for a godly husband, strive to become the kind of woman her future spouse would want, make her involvement in her church a higher priority than her career, dedicate herself to various forms of volunteer service (perhaps with children, crisis pregnancy centers, and so on), and endeavor to make her friends in the world of families rather than the realm of "career singles."

If moving back home is not a realistic option, Denise should maintain a positive and close relationship with her father. If a man decides he is interested in Denise, that young man should call her father and become acquainted with him and then share his intentions. Although it is long distance, this interaction can help the father get to know this young man and decide whether he is right for his daughter or not. As a pastor of a number of unmarried college students who are committed to the courtship model and live away from home, I have seen this pattern work well a number of times.

THE PRESENT DISTRESS

It is impossible to get too far into a discussion like this without certain Scripture passages coming to mind. And we start asking ourselves, *I wonder how that relates to this?* One of the passages that commonly comes to mind is 1 Corinthians 7 because in it, the apostle Paul spends a good deal of time talking about men and women.

However, in order to understand many of his instructions, we have to get the context right. In this passage, there is one fundamental contextual issue of importance: the point in history when Paul was writing. Paul knew that the church was coming up on a significant time of persecution—the persecution in which he ended up losing his life. The emperor Nero attacked the church savagely during this time (AD 64–68), and Paul knew that it would not be easy to take care of a family. He therefore urged the saints to travel light. He said, "I suppose therefore that this is good because of the present distress—that it is good for a man to remain as he is" (7:26). The "present distress" was the climate in which Paul was giving his counsel. We should understand it accordingly, and when we are facing comparable circumstances, we should take note of what Paul urged. It is one thing to refuse to deny Christ and be thrown to the lions. It is quite another to refuse to deny Christ and see your young wife and three-year-old daughter thrown to the lions.

Throughout history, there have been many times when marriage was not the wisest course of action, and this is the principle we should take from this passage. For example, a soldier should not get married two days before he is scheduled to leave for war—unless he is afraid of sexual sin in those two days. Paul's advice was due to the present distress. When there is no present distress but rather a lovely garden with a tire swing, the Lord God says, "It is not good that man should be alone" (Genesis 2:18).

PREHEATING THE OVEN

In the passage from 1 Corinthians 7 already discussed, we see that in this fallen world, protection against sexual immorality is one of the reasons for marriage: "Nevertheless, because of sexual immorality, let each man have his own wife, and let each woman have her own husband" (verse 2). This is obviously not the only purpose for marriage, but it is one of them.

Knowing this, we have to realize that sexual attraction is indeed important. The marriage bed is to be honored by Christians (see Hebrews 13:4), and part of this honor includes approaching that bed happily with sexual desire. Biblical lovers are invited to be intoxicated with one another's lovemaking (see Song of Solomon 5:1). The wine of the marriage bed should not be something that has to be choked down. Not to belabor the obvious, but this high view of lovemaking is not possible if the man and woman do not find one another sexually attractive. Too many young Christians think that such motives are somehow biblically unworthy, but this is far removed from the truth. Marriage is a covenanted sexual relationship.

When a guy singles out a young woman in some romantic fashion, this means that one of two things is happening. Either he is trying to get her into bed dishonorably, or he is attempting to get her into bed honorably. In either case, there is a sexual element involved. Incidentally, this illustrates yet another advantage of the courtship model. When a young man is approaching a young woman, she can kid herself about the nature of his interest for a long time. But if he approaches her father, her father knows exactly what is going on. Dad will be much harder to persuade that the young man has suddenly developed a spontaneous interest in flowers.

God's will for us includes being sexually sanctified. Paul addresses this in 1 Thessalonians:

> For this is the will of God, your sanctification: that you should abstain from sexual immorality; that each of you should know how to possess his own vessel in sanctification and honor, not in passion of lust, like the Gentiles who do not know God; that no one should take advantage of and defraud his brother in this matter, because the Lord is the avenger of all such, as we also forewarned you and testified. For God did not call us to uncleanness, but in holiness. (4:3-7)

It is unclear whether a man's "own vessel" refers to his own body or to the body of his wife, but in this case it is fortunate that either interpretation amounts to the same thing. A Christian man needs to approach a woman sexually in a manner distinct from what unbelievers do.

Another problem exists when an unmarried couple sleeps together and then later marries one another. This scenario erodes trust between husband and wife. Both of them know that the law of God did not restrain the other in the presence of temptation. They know this because they were there. Let's assume they are now married, and the husband is off on a business trip. His wife knows his weaknesses firsthand—that practicing sexual self-control is hard for him. The seeds of distrust have been well planted.

Therefore, I believe that in the courtship process before there is any covenant commitment, there should be zero physical involvement. The couple is getting to know one another at this stage and deciding whether they want to give themselves to one another. They should not give themselves while still deciding whether or not they want to.

Once the woman's father gives the man permission to seek his daughter's hand in marriage and the couple is engaged, I believe there are two dangers to avoid. One illustration I use concerning this is that of unrolling a carpet. A full, intimate marriage relationship is like an unrolled Persian carpet. Some couples, even after they are engaged, have virtually no physical contact (though they may because engagement is a covenantal commitment at some level). This means that on their wedding night, they unroll the whole thing, which can lead to unfortunate results. A couple who has never communicated to one another their sexual expectations can discover, much to their mutual dismay, that their expectations were completely different. And this can mean that what should have been a joyful consummation is actually the beginning of a long marital struggle. If she has a hazy romantic gauze covering the lens of her mental camera, and he has wild and crazy sexual interests, the results can be really unfortunate.

At the same time, too much communication presents additional sexual temptations for an engaged couple. Moderation is important. I would suggest that a couple pace themselves according to how far away the wedding is and that they limit themselves to holding hands, kisses, and hugs of affection and stay away from anything that would count as foreplay. When couples unroll the whole carpet except for the last foot and a half and then try to hang on for the remaining four months until the wedding, it can get very dangerous. To use a different metaphor, if it is not time to cook the roast, don't preheat the oven.

HEADSHIP AND SUBMISSION

It should be obvious by now that I am rejecting the egalitarian approach to familial relationships, particularly the relationship between parents and daughters and also between husbands and wives. But how does this square with Paul's glorious statement: "For as many of you as were baptized into Christ have put on Christ. There is neither Jew nor Greek, there is neither slave nor free, there is neither male nor female; for you are all one in Christ Jesus" (Galatians 3:27-28)? If there is neither male nor female in Christ, then how can we assign all these various responsibilities based on gender? Isn't this disparaging wives and daughters? Why do sons get to leave? Why do daughters have to be given?

There are two responses to this: Headship is not what most people assume it to be, and neither is submission. The caricature of headship is that of a bossy man demanding food and sex when and where he wants it. The caricature of submission is that of a mousy wife acting the role of compliant doormat.

But the real model for headship is Jesus Christ: "For the husband is head of the wife, as also Christ is head of the church; and He is the Savior of the body" (Ephesians 5:23). Husbands are called to love their wives as Christ loved the church; He gave Himself up for her. This means that husbands are summoned to a life of sacrifice. Jesus showed His authority among His disciples—and it was true authority—by washing their feet. This is the kingdom ethic. Does anyone want to be great in the kingdom? Then he must be the servant of all. It is no different in the home. All Christian authority follows this model, the example of Jesus. The husband who would be the authority in his home must exercise that authority through godly service. Obviously, a daughter who has grown up in a home where her father has treated her mother and her in this way is a daughter who can trust her father when it comes to courtship.

In the same way, the duty of submission is not fulfilled by wives and daughters cowering in the corner. The Bible teaches that husbands are to love their wives with understanding, treating them as the weaker vessel. Peter instructs, "Husbands, likewise, dwell with them with understanding, giving honor to the wife, as to the weaker vessel, and as being heirs together of the grace of life, that your prayers may not be hindered (1 Peter 3:7). But this requires explanation. Too often men read this passage and unfortunately respond to it with a junior-high mentality. Thinking of every difference in terms of competition, they start doing a little touchdown dance. "My wife loses! I am the strong one!" But this response just proves, among other things, that the men can't read. Peter assumes that the information he is providing will lead men to *honor* their wives.

A china vase is weaker than a backhoe. But it is superior to the backhoe for a whole range of activities. And the backhoe is better for others. Our triune God did not create differences in the world so that we could try to figure out whether the sun or moon is better.

This means that daughters who grow up in a godly home know they are far superior to their father and brothers in the role God has assigned to them. And the father and brothers are superior in the role God has given them. Reasonable people wouldn't try to arrange flowers in a backhoe, nor would they try to dig a ditch with a vase. God's design for the world makes sense. Trying to ignore the features He built into men and women makes no sense at all. But even though we are each superior in our roles, we are equal in value. As Paul said, we are all one in Christ.

| **What Do You Think?** | Douglas suggests certain differences between men and women. Do you agree with his statements? |

I have had the great privilege of spending my life around women who are known for their godly submission to their husbands—my mother, my wife, my sister, and my daughters. The idea that some pushy male could walk up, thump his chest a few times, and browbeat any of them amuses me greatly. I would like to be there when he tries it.

THE WILL OF GOD, OR THE PROBLEM OF SUZY LORDSCHOICE

The questions that arise concerning the will of God are pronounced in the courtship process because those involved know they are making monumentally important decisions. And decision making and the will of God is a large theological area involving many factors. For the sake of space, this brief discussion will have to do.

First, many evangelical Christians are, in my view, mistaken about the nature of the will of God when they try to get an agenda beforehand from the Lord. In this approach, living and walking in the will of God becomes little more than a pagan form of fortune-telling. We want God to throw a brick through our front window with a note tied to it, saying, "Marry him" or "Marry her." But God does not lead us in this way.

James warns us against arrogance when it comes to the future:

> Come now, you who say, "Today or tomorrow we will go to such and such a city, spend a year there, buy and sell, and make a profit"; whereas you do not know what will happen tomorrow. For what is your life? It is even a vapor that appears for a little time and then vanishes away. Instead you ought to say, "If the Lord wills, we shall live and do this or that." But now you boast in your arrogance. All such boasting is evil. (4:13-16)

Consequently, apart from special revelation (which includes, of course, God's Word), to claim that something is God's will can be arrogance. Unfortunately, this is something many young Christian men have done to young women. An attractive young woman joins the college and career group at church, and all of a sudden about ten guys start hearing from the Holy Spirit. Most men would take a stiff drink before they approach a woman. But Christian men think they are called to "seek the will of God." And yet, it is manifestly unfair and presumptuous for a man to approach a young woman and use the will of God as a tool of manipulation. In such situations, the will of God is actually being used as a club, which is utterly inconsistent with the law of charity. If the young lady is not interested in the man who has approached her in this way, she can be accused of being unspiritual.

What Do You Think? How do you react to Douglas's comments about God's will? Have you ever claimed that you should pursue a dating relationship with someone because you believed it was God's will? Compared to what Douglas says, how does your situation apply?

I believe that we are responsible for living out the will of God, but we are not called upon to determine it beforehand. I have been happily married for twenty-nine years, but I still do not know if it is God's will for me to be married tomorrow. I or my wife or both of us may go to be with the Lord. Our lives are a mist, and mist ought not make dogmatic pronouncements about how it will fare tomorrow.

This being the case, what should we do to walk in the will of God? If we are not supposed to obtain a divine schedule and then follow it, how are we to approach this? In the context of courtship, the first thing to do is make sure that the general will of God as it is revealed in the Bible is being carefully honored. If one of the persons is divorced, was it a lawful divorce? Are parents being honored in the pursuit of courtship? In short form, it is never the will of God to court your next-door neighbor's wife, your sister, or the fourteen-year-old daughter of godly and disapproving parents.

When the revealed will of God for all Christians is being honored, what is our responsibility after that? We have a great responsibility to conduct our lives, including this aspect, with wisdom. I counsel young people to consider three basic questions as they attempt to do that: What are your abilities? What are your opportunities? What are your desires?

Family and friends who know you best can help you answer these questions, although some questions may be settled only in time alone with God. A man might be interested in a woman for whom he is not able to provide. Those counseling him should urge him to consider that more carefully than perhaps he otherwise would. Or perhaps a woman has shut a suitor down repeatedly, and he is just not getting the message. He has no opportunity, and wisdom should see that. But if a man is able and has the opportunity, then what should he do? The Bible tells us,

> Delight yourself also in the LORD,
> And He shall give you the desires of your heart.
>
> (Psalm 37:4)

He should seek out the woman he is able to love, the one who would respond to him favorably, the one who is the delight of his eyes. And she should make decisions in the same way.

PLATONIC RELATIONSHIPS?

Are platonic relationships between men and women possible? By platonic, I mean a relationship between a man and a woman in which all romantic and erotic elements are absent. To this I would give this qualified answer: "Not really." And if we remove the really odd, entirely unlikely situations, such as a seventeen-year-old boy befriending a ninety-two-year-old woman, I would answer, "Not at all."

Many years ago at the beginning of my ministry, I resolved to make friends with no women apart from my wife, mother, sister, and daughters. My wife and I together may be friends with another couple, a single man, or a single woman—and we enjoy such friendships. But when a man and a woman get together in a way that pairs them off, I think that to say they are "just friends" is an instance of one or both of them kidding themselves. And the fact that one of them knows that the other "would never be interested in me romantically in a million years" does nothing to prevent him or her from getting attached to the other and being unable to say anything about it because they already agreed that they are "just friends."

ONE SIZE FITS ALL? OR HOW MIGHT THE COURTSHIP MODEL GO WRONG?

We have to remember that we live in a sinful world and that all methods of action are simply attempts to accommodate this unfortunate reality in various ways. This means that courtship is a system that deals with sinful and selfish people, some more so than others. And this in turn means that not every courtship story will end in harmony. I have heard some awful ones. But the problems that arise do not arise because of courtship but rather because of sins such as dishonesty, lust, a domineering spirit, and so on. This is also the problem in the other models discussed in this volume. The problem is not the model; the problem is the people. And so the question that faces those who are arguing for one model over the other is not whether or not people will sin in the name of this model. The question is which model best anticipates and guards against the inevitable sin. And the answer to that question, in my opinion, is the courtship model.

But when the courtship model is abused, in what ways is that abuse likely to manifest itself? Allow me to mention just a few problem areas.

Overzealous Expectations of Others

Those who have come out of a tangled history of recreational dating are frequently tempted to assume that everyone else is as passionate about courtship as they are, and they end up becoming total nuisances. For example, a young woman who has been through fifteen casual dating relationships and then has been "delivered" from that approach might throw a fit if a friend of hers was thinking about going on just one date with an interested young man. Whether such a date is a good idea is certainly debatable — but the "new woman" should not be overzealous in her expectations of her friend.

Controlling Parents

Domineering fathers and manipulative mothers are frequently tempted to use the courtship model as a way of controlling their children instead of serving them.

Sometimes parents who get involved in the courtship process believe that because the model is biblical, every nitpicky decision that has to be made must be biblical, too. And this is how legalism starts. For example, some might say that God requires a courting couple to sit no closer than eighteen inches from one another on the third visit to the young woman's house. It can get over the top very quickly.

Faking Courtship

One last problem occurs when courtship becomes "whatever we want to do," which is no real practice of the method but is still called courtship. Young couples should realize that the courtship method exists for their good and isn't just a cool or on-the-surface "Christian" label. This couple should spend time praying about the way they will conduct their relationship, and obviously, they should include their parents in an honest discussion about it.

THE WAY COURTSHIP WORKS IN REAL LIFE

Here's an example of an ideal courtship: Luke has been interested in Jamie for about six months. He recently returned home after graduating from college, and he's found a good job. He has known Jamie for six years because they both went to the local Christian high school. Since he has been back, he has found himself strongly attracted to her. He does not know if this is simply because he is ready to get married or if he's really into Jamie.

After a period of several months, during which his attraction to her did not settle down and he found himself frequently and nonchalantly drifting over to visit with whatever group she was in after church, he sought out his parents' counsel. They all sat down and went over his circumstances, which resulted in their encouraging him to talk with Jamie's father. They had admired Jamie as a young woman in the church for some time and were delighted with Luke's interest. They also were pleased that Luke had done well in school and in his new job and was clearly responsible enough to provide for a family.

Luke approached Jamie's father, Jim, the next week at church, and they scheduled a lunch for the following day. When they got down to business, Luke told him that he had been interested in Jamie for six months and wanted Jim's blessing to get to know her better. When Jim pressed him, Luke acknowledged that he was "fairly settled" in what he wanted to do. In other words, he was not interested in finding a girlfriend but would like to court Jamie with marriage in mind. He understood that Jamie was not in the same confident position and so it would be more likely for her to call the courtship off than it would be for him.

Jim sincerely thanked Luke for the way he was pursuing his daughter and told him he would pray about it, talk to his wife and to Jamie, and get back to him within a few days. That evening, Jim and his wife, Laurie, sat down with Jamie and talked through the idea. Jamie respected Luke greatly but had no idea why he would be interested in her. This told Jim and Laurie that one of the key elements in a successful marriage (respect) was already present in her. She was attracted to him and very interested, but she was unsure about whether she knew enough to do anything. "That is what courtship is for," Jim said, and so Jamie agreed.

The next day, Jim called Luke at work and told him he had his permission to take Jamie out to dinner and to come over to their house afterward to hang out. And that is the kind of thing they did for the next several months—an occasional date, a lot of dinners with Jamie's family, and lots of good conversation. During this time, Jim and Laurie periodically visited with Jamie. As time unfolded, she told them she was more and more impressed with Luke. This was fortunate because Jim and Laurie felt exactly the same way. Finally, Jim asked his daughter one evening what she would say if Luke proposed to her. She said she would be delighted to say yes.

The following day, Jim called Luke and asked if he was free for lunch. When they got together, Jim asked if Luke was still of the same mind that he had been when the courtship began. He was—enthusiastically so. During the last several months, he had gone from being attracted to Jamie to falling in love with her. As he put it to Jim, every night when he got home, he would look at a picture of Jamie on his end table and then "roll on the floor, chew the carpet, and howl at the moon." Jim told

Luke that he had his and Laurie's blessing to take Jamie out for a special dinner and give her a ring.

And so he did. And they lived happily ever after, just like in the stories.

THE COURTSHIP PATH: AN OVERVIEW

Definition

Courtship is the active, involved authority of the young woman's father (or head of the household) in the formation of her romantic attachments leading to marriage.

Distinctives

- Courtship is not egalitarian because it believes in a female submission to a male head of the home.

- If there is an absence of headship, either because of neglect or a literal absence, young couples should seek out advice from their church on how to continue their courtship. This will probably result in an assignment of surrogate parents.

- Physical involvement when courting should be completely avoided. After the couple is engaged, it should be limited to holding hands, brief kisses, and hugs.

- The will of God is rarely an acceptable excuse to conduct courtship in a self-defined way, such as a man pursuing a woman who has repeatedly rejected his interest in her.

- Platonic relationships are a myth and are not an excuse to spend one-on-one time with a member of the opposite sex outside of courtship.

Key Verses

- Numbers 30:3-5

- Genesis 2:18

- Psalm 37:4

Key Benefits

- Love develops within a supportive, protective, and encouraging environment.

- Sexual purity is more realistic and attainable.

- Trust in the relationship results because intentions are more obvious from the get-go.

- Baggage occurs less often because all aspects of the relationship are more intentional.

- Courtship creates an environment for obeying God by honoring one's parents.

Potential Problems

- Courtshippers may become overzealous to the point of forcing their method on others.

- Parents may become domineering and manipulative, using the authority of courtship to make unwise, ungodly decisions in all areas of their children's lives.

- Couples may claim they are courting to appear Christian but may ignore the real principles and make up their own unhealthy rules.

THE GUIDED PATH 3

Rick Holland

THEY WERE UPSET — *REALLY* UPSET! AFTER I FINISHED PREACHING that Sunday morning, they charged me like I was a matador.

"Rick, don't you think dating is wrong? Isn't courtship the way they did it in the Bible?"

Before I could answer, another girl instantly added, "Rick, the word *courtship* isn't even in the Bible, is it? And God never says that dating is wrong, right?"

I am a pastor of nearly one thousand collegians in the Los Angeles area. LA is a college town like few others. Over fifteen colleges and universities are represented in our ministry, and many of these students come to our church from a variety of backgrounds. Each brings a set of ideas about how to do relationships. I think it is fair to say that we have just about seen it all when it comes to ideas about romance.

The above interchange characterizes much of what's happening in the great dating debate. Many people are more passionate about the process they use than the person God has called them to be. Oftentimes, method is emphasized over theology; process is emphasized over personal maturity; and premarital methodology, which is short-term, is emphasized over marital understanding, which is long-term.

The collision of ideologies about how to do premarital relationships can be ugly. I saw it on the faces of those two college girls who approached me that Sunday morning. I had no choice but to decide what I believe about relationships and romance and unabashedly teach it. This chapter summarizes what I've concluded.

Each contributor to this volume has been invited to participate because of a commitment to conducting relationships biblically. But the fact that you are holding this book is evidence that there is no consensus on what that means. The number of books promoting models and methods for acquiring a spouse grows almost monthly. Perusing the relationships section of a Christian bookstore is much like walking through the cereal aisle at the grocery store. New options seem to show up every time you visit.

All that said, I believe we can learn and apply much from each of the relationship models presented in this book. But I also believe it is unwise to conclude that the Bible prescribes a specific blueprint for finding your one and only.

A CLOSER LOOK AT THE DATING CONTROVERSY

What is good about this debate is that Christians are taking dating and romance seriously. The controversy has forced us all to evaluate the source of our beliefs. Even better, it has launched a reengagement with the Bible as the authority for whom and how we marry.

As with many discussions about biblical issues, the dating debate has involved some unfortunate elements. One example is the problem of definitions. Not all in the dating camp agree on what dating actually is and what regulates its standards. It is not fair to categorize all dating ideologies as the same (as is true in this book). In many books and websites that criticize dating from a Christian perspective, seldom is it admitted that dating could be approached in a way that honors God. Often the criticism is built on worst-case-scenario dating relationships. And those in the courtship/betrothal camp have no consensus on what courtship is either. Try reading the courtship books by Douglas Wilson, Josh Harris, and Paul Jehle back-to-back.[1] These courting approaches have much in common, but they also include some major differences. Unfortunately, most books and websites assume there is agreement on the meaning of terms.

In reality, there exists a spectrum of beliefs within each relational model. Not all courtship systems are the same. And the term *dating* can refer to anything from sharing a cup of coffee to a serious relationship.

THE PLACE TO START

The Bible is to be the ultimate source for "all things that pertain to life and godliness" (2 Peter 1:3).[2] As such, it is the sole source for what God thinks, commands, ordains, and allows for man, the crowning glory of His creation. But most of us also know that the Bible never mentions dating, nor does it mention courtship. You can search any Bible concordance in vain to find either of these words in even a single verse. You will find the words *betrothed* or *engaged* in Scripture. But because they are used either in passages regulating Israel's family structure or in describing the situation in a narrative account, it is challenging to apply their specifics today. And though Christians are in a covenant relationship with the Savior before we are spiritually married to Him (see Revelation 19:9), there is no biblical command to use an ancient Near Eastern betrothal contract to obtain a spouse.

But God's Word does discuss premarital relationships. At the risk of overgeneralizing, those who hold to a dating method approach these passages more generally, drawing out principles from these texts, while those who hold to a courtship/betrothal method approach these same passages more specifically, drawing out practices. So the significant difference between the two approaches lies in the specificity with which the scriptural data can be applied.

The question that really underlies the dating debate is how to apply the *prescriptions* about getting married that we read in the Law (Genesis through Deuteronomy) and the *descriptions* of relationships in the narratives, or stories. This is not a simple question to answer. For example, is it legitimate to see the commands in the Law concerning premarital relationships as binding, while leaving other commands strangely unapplied? I have yet to see a strong argument made for paying a poor worker every day instead of every payday. But that is what the Law commands (see Deuteronomy 24:14-15). And what about narrative literature? Why do some argue that we should imitate the Isaac story in Genesis 24,[3] but few—if any—suggest that the pattern in Ruth 3 should be an example? Ruth waits until Boaz goes to sleep, lies down by his feet, and proposes when he wakes up!

My point is this: No matter which method you propose, it is more complicated than it sounds. The thing is, who would argue with a system in which godly parents partner with godly children to pair up godly couples for godly marriages as they do in betrothal and courtship? It sounds too good to be true. Sometimes it is not—the system can work just as it sounds, resulting in God being glorified and marriages being enjoyed. But for courting to really work, many intricate pieces need to come together in perfect harmony. Two sets of parents and two singles need to be on the same page about the system and about each other.

I will admit it. If courting worked out in practice the way it looks on paper, you could count me in. But what concerns me most about the courtship movement as I've seen it is that it lends itself to a strange form of idolatry. Advocates of courtship are understandably passionate about their system—so much so that they often try to convert daters to courters with an evangelistic zeal. Unintentionally, the courting system itself can become so important to courters that God is deemphasized.

On the other hand, while courting and betrothal are often selective in applying Scripture, many dating models ignore or neglect major biblical principles. Dating relationships typically operate with few thought-out guidelines. Many who date take a largely passive approach. And few who date could give a biblical justification for what they are doing. Often the issue is not one of interpreting the Bible; they are not even using the Bible. Sadly, much of the literature describing and defending dating is built more on love stories than biblical instruction.[4]

Not all dating relationships or the books promoting them are bad or unbiblical. It is an unfair and unfounded criticism of dating to say that if one dates, one is sinning. Nowhere does the Bible indicate that an unengaged couple spending time together is a sin—unless they are committing fornication. Countless couples have enjoyed Christ-exalting marriages resulting from Christ-honoring dating relationships. Who you are in your character as a result of being in Christ is more important than whether you date or court. Josh Harris's thoughts are helpful:

> What I hope you see is that avoiding lawlessness and legalism is far more important than whether we use the word *dating* or the word *courtship*.
>
> I happen to like the term *courtship*. It's old-fashioned, but it evokes romance and chivalry. I use it to describe not a set of rules, but that special *season* in a romance where a man and woman are seriously weighing the

possibility of marriage. I think it's helpful to distinguish between undefined and directionless romances (what I said goodbye to) and a romantic relationship that is purposefully headed towards marriage. But the fact that I use the word *courtship* to describe my relationship with Shannon doesn't make me holier than people who don't.

None of us should allow a debate over words to distract us from what really matters in relationships. "Dating versus courtship" isn't the point. I've known "serial courters" who lived like the devil and "saintly daters" guided by integrity and holiness. In and of themselves, the terms they used to describe their relationships were meaningless. The way they lived is what really mattered. Terms don't define our lives; our lives define our terms.[5]

Additionally, Doug Wilson writes, "Being married *amplifies* what a person is."[6] If you are the right kind of person, are looking for the right kind of person, and pleasing Christ is your highest priority, the method you use is secondary.

THE GUIDED APPROACH

The approach I take to dating relationships is called "guided." I call it this because people who follow it are guided through relationships by honoring principles given in the Bible. But I want to make it clear: These are guidelines, not formulas.

The New Testament addresses a battle for balance between two extreme approaches to godliness: legalism and libertinism. These two extremes have a parallel in the dating debate. Dating without a plan can easily become too loose. Courting without wisdom can easily become legalism. In its extreme, dating becomes an anything-goes free-for-all in which the man and woman concern themselves with the pleasure of the romance instead of the good of each other. Courting in its extreme becomes an infatuation with a process instead of an evaluation using biblical principles.

THE PURPOSE OF PREMARITAL RELATIONSHIPS

Premarital relationships should serve one purpose: to test the relationship for marriage. Let me say it another way: *There is no good reason to have a girlfriend or boyfriend until a person is ready to get married!* I hope the implications of this statement are obvious. Readiness involves being old enough and mature enough to assume the responsibilities of marriage. No romantic relationship should ever begin unless marriage is the possible—even probable—outcome. That said, it is difficult to justify the romances of junior high and high school. If one is not ready to get married, he or she is not ready to date or court.

So what about Jenny and David? They are juniors in high school. They are both Christians and involved in their church. Both get that funny feeling in their stomachs when they are around each other. Add to that their friends' constant nagging about them making a good couple. What should they do?

This may not be what they want to hear, but they should forget about it! No romantic relationship should be developed unless the couple can get married if all goes well. If they are not ready to get married, they are not ready to date. Dating without marriage on the radar is an unnecessarily risky business.

Jenny and David should continue to cultivate good, biblical friendships with each other—and with others—as spiritual siblings. But I would encourage them to wait until they are ready to get married before they consider dating.

So if you are not ready to be married, how can you get ready? Whether you are too young or too immature to enter into a relationship that could lead to marriage, a path to a God-honoring marriage can be paved if you will look to God's Word.

I believe that the following ten principles can help any person in any context honor God's relational values and in turn become a godly person ready for a godly relationship. In fact, these guidelines can be followed regardless of the model you choose.

TEN PRINCIPLES FOR A GOD-CENTERED RELATIONSHIP

1. The Character Principle

It is the pattern and practice of God to judge a man or woman's true character by looking inside at what is in the heart (see 1 Samuel 16:7). Externals reveal only so much about the true person. If we are to be faithful imitators of our heavenly Father, evaluation of a potential spouse should be based first on character.

The Character Principle is about *being* the right person more than *finding* the right person. If your character is being conformed more and more into the image of Christ, you will desire the right kind of person. There are numerous texts informing the believer how to live a life that pleases God. The second chapter of Titus is an exemplary passage that gives a blueprint for training the character of succeeding generations. Because it speaks to both men and women, it provides a succinct summary of what God desires for our lives.

Paul was instructing Titus on how to put things in order in the church (see Titus 1:5). An important part of getting the church in order was to ensure that older believers were discipling younger believers to be men and women of godly character. Much of the apostle's instruction to Titus as both a pastor and a young man was directly related to relationships. As he addressed the older men and women, a clear *example* of godly character came into view. And as he spoke about the next generation, a clear *exhortation* of godly character emerged:

> Older men are to be sober-minded, dignified, self-controlled, sound in faith, in love, and in steadfastness. Older women likewise are to be reverent in behavior, not slanderers or slaves to much wine. They are to teach what is good, and so train the young women to love their husbands and children, to be self-controlled, pure, working at home, kind, and submissive to their own husbands, that the word of God may not be reviled. Likewise, urge the younger men to be self-controlled. Show yourself in all respects to be a model of good works, and in your teaching show integrity, dignity, and sound speech that cannot be condemned, so that an opponent may be put to shame, having nothing evil to say about us. (Titus 2:2-8)

Notice that godly character is a product of spiritual discipleship. One of the best ways to prepare for a marital relationship is to maintain a mentoring relationship with an older, wiser, and godlier member of the same sex.

In addition to what Paul told Titus, godly character consists of qualities such as humility (see Philippians 2:3-11), holiness (see 1 Peter 1:14-16), godly love (see 1 Corinthians 13:4-8), selflessness (see James 3:14), the fruit of the Spirit (see Galatians 5:22-25), and, of course, Christlikeness (see Ephesians 4:13).

The Character Principle has another dimension: recognition. Not only should godly character be pursued personally, but it should also be recognized in anyone a person might date or court. King Lemuel crystallized the Character Principle with his contrasting words:

> Charm is deceitful, and beauty is vain,
> but a woman who fears the LORD is to be praised.
>
> (Proverbs 31:30)

2. The Confirmation Principle

One of the many potholes of recreational dating is that it often finds affirmation and confirmation from the wrong sources. I know that many who date submit themselves humbly and willingly to the authorities in their lives, but sadly, many others do not. The Confirmation Principle is the commitment to submit one's life and relationships to the spiritual scrutiny of God's authority, care, and protection represented here on earth. Who are these authorities? Let me outline three.

Parental Confirmation. God has given parents authority over their children (see Exodus 20:12; Leviticus 19:3; Deuteronomy 21:18-21; 27:16; Matthew 15:4; Romans 1:28-32; Ephesians 6:1-2; 2 Timothy 3:1-5). Therefore, to ignore this authority is to ignore God. But what does this mean in premarital relationships?

First, parents should be involved from the beginning. Many parents desire to be involved with all aspects of a relationship in the initial stages, including who is to be pursued and considered for marriage. Unfortunately, some do not. Regardless, it should be the heart of a son or daughter to submit his or her decisions about relationships to his or her parents. This involves getting their thoughts, listening to their concerns, proceeding at their pace, and applying the brakes if they say, "Wait" or "Stop." But what if you and your parents disagree? Ravi Zacharias shares this wisdom: "The chances are that if you marry someone in violation of your parents' will, you are playing a high-stakes game as you enter your new future. Any time you violate an authority that has been put in place by God, you need to be twice as sure you are doing the right thing."[7] How can you know if you are doing the right thing? There is another level of authority.

Church Affirmation. One of the most neglected sources of wisdom in the Christian life is church leaders. Pastors, elders, deacons, and other leaders should be intricately involved in any budding relationship. This is especially important if the parents are deceased, far away, or out of the picture for other reasons. It is a curious fact that more is said in the Bible about the role of church leaders in our lives than even the role of our parents (see Ephesians 4:11-16; 1 Timothy; 2 Timothy; Titus; Hebrews 13:7,17). Only a fool would disregard this arm of God's authority.

I am often asked what should be done if there is a disagreement among children and their parents about relational issues. Paul answers this in principle in 1 Corinthians 6. Two believers were having a disagreement they could not resolve, and it resulted in a lawsuit. As the apostle shames them for appealing to a secular court, he makes the passing comment that disputes among believers ought to be resolved by wise leaders in the church (see 1 Corinthians 6:4-6). This is true of relational disagreements as well.

What should you do if your plan for your life and romance differs from your parents'? Let me offer some guidelines for honoring your parents when you disagree with them.[8]

Be prayerful, humble, and ready to be corrected by their concerns. Don't assume that they are wrong and you are right.

Try to be as objective as possible in evaluating the relationship in light of biblical principles instead of your emotional desires. When emotions are high, good judgment is rarely present. Discuss the disagreement in a respectful way. God gives parents—Christian *and* non-Christian ones—wisdom and instruction. Remember, there are no qualifications in the fifth commandment.

If there is no resolution, seek counsel—with them if possible—from church leaders. When you seek counsel, never speak of your parents in a way that is dishonoring to them. Seek to change your heart rather than your parents! Only go against your parents when all biblical and church resources have been exhausted and the church leadership counsels you in that direction.

We live in the world of Bart Simpson, a world in which obeying and honoring parents is considered uncool and even archaic. But this very fact should bring us all to our knees.

Friend Affirmation. A third source of wisdom to affirm your relationship is godly friends. The book of Proverbs exhorts us to listen to wise counsel around us (see 12:15; 15:22; 19:20-21; 27:9). The insights and observations of mature Christian friends should add yet another layer of accountability in relational decisions. One of the mistakes we often make is listening only to counsel with which we agree. But if we have the right kind of friends, their biblical wisdom, as well as the work of the Holy Spirit in their lives, can be a strong ally to help us make relational decisions, whether it is what we want to hear or not.

The Confirmation Principle invites God's grace into complicated situations. For Steve and Rachel, it could be invaluable. As collegians, they are not living at home. Their families are not only far away, but they are also unbelievers. Yet Steve and Rachel find godly qualities in one another and are attracted to each other. How should they proceed?

Even though their parents are not Christians, seeking their confirmation is wise and obedient. I believe God would honor their efforts to seek their counsel and wisdom. But what if that is not helpful? What if their parents' insights are ungodly and dishonoring to Scripture?

This is where pastoral oversight becomes critical. I would never encourage a couple to go against their parents' counsel (even if the parents are unbelievers) without a serious evaluation and oversight by pastors and elders. And the counsel of other mature believers can also be used by God to put the relationship under the microscope.

Steve and Rachel should move forward in the relationship only after they have exhausted the confirmation possible from their parents, pastors, and friends.

3. The Contentment Principle

The foundation for developing a righteous relationship with a member of the opposite sex is the ultimate relationship—your relationship with God. If you are not happy with God alone, you will not be happy with someone else. Paul's walk with Christ was so satisfying that he discovered that contentment was possible regardless of any circumstance (see Philippians 4:10-13; 1 Timothy 6:6-7).

A huge error singles often make is believing that a relationship will make them happy. This is just another form of idolatry. Thinking that anything other than God will bring satisfaction and happiness is to make that object an idol in one's life. Stacy, a friend of mine, used to spend inestimable time dreaming and pining about a relationship. My wife and I spoke to her many times about the fact that a boyfriend would not bring the happiness she thought it would.

Finally, it happened. She met a guy who became her friend and eventually her boyfriend. Stacy put her whole life into the relationship. On the surface, she could have won the girlfriend-of-the-year award. Then something amazing happened: engagement!

Everything looked great on the outside. But about two months into her marriage, she began to skip church and slip into despair. When I had a chance to talk with her, her honesty was shocking. She told me, "Rick, I really thought a man would bring me happiness. Now I have one. He's a great husband, and I know he will be a loving father. But I am lonelier now than when I was single. What is my problem?"

Stacy's problem was that her contentment was built on a person rather than on God. If you struggle with discontentment now, you will struggle with discontentment when you are married. Discontentment is a sin. It should be recognized and repented of long before a relationship begins.

But don't misunderstand. Strong desire to have a relationship does not necessarily mean discontentment is present. It is noble and God-honoring to want a godly relationship and marriage. But the line is crossed if you start to feel sorry for yourself because you don't have a relationship, become jealous of those who do have a relationship, compromise or sin in order to obtain a relationship, or become frustrated with God because you are dateless. God is *for* us! Remember His promise in Psalm 84:11:

> For the LORD God is a sun and shield;
> the LORD bestows favor and honor.

No good thing does he withhold
from those who walk uprightly.

If we walk with Him, we can trust God's providence to bring us what is good and keep from us what is not. This includes relationships. If you are not currently in a relationship, it might be that God does not see it as a good thing for you at this time. The psalmist tells us that the path to blessing is to "walk uprightly" (see the Character Principle). Marriage is not the solution to the discontentment you feel being single. Matrimony can never replace Jesus as the fulfillment of your heart's desire.

What Do You Think? | How do you feel about Rick's comment, "If you are not currently in a relationship, it might be that God does not see it as a good thing for you at this time"?

4. The Common Ground Principle

A Christian should consider only another Christian for a romantic relationship and marriage. Second Corinthians 6:14-18 teaches that believers and unbelievers mix no better than light and darkness. The Holy Spirit could not have been clearer. A Christian is not to be yoked with an unbeliever in any spiritual enterprise. And there is no such enterprise more important than marriage. God commands those who are seeking to be married to do so only "in the Lord" (1 Corinthians 7:39).

The point, then, is simple: *Don't marry an unbeliever!* And if marrying an unbeliever is not God's will, then dating one is also out of bounds. Pursuing a relationship with an unbeliever is the most serious mistake you can make in this area. If you do not choose a person who has a living, breathing relationship with the Lord, there is disaster in your future (see 1 Kings 11:1-3).

What Do You Think?	Rick says, "*Don't marry an unbeliever!* And if marrying an unbeliever is not God's will, then dating one is also out of bounds." Do you agree? Why or why not?

I have heard so many justifications for dating unbelievers. But the most creative one is called missionary dating. The idea is that dating an unbeliever is a great way to expose them to Christ. I mean, think about it, how much more access can you have to a person's heart than through a romance? Nice idea, but unwise.

Other Christians enter into relationships with unbelievers because of their desire for a relationship. You know how this one goes. There is a nice Christian girl who is faithful at church, but no Christian guy shows any interest in her. Then it happens. She is sitting in her economics class her freshman year of college, and the cute guy sitting in front of her asks her out. She knows he is not a Christian, but her desire for a relationship elbows her wisdom out of the way—and an unequally yoked relationship is born.

Do you remember what happened to Solomon? He disobeyed God by marrying women from foreign lands with foreign idols. Solomon was considered the wisest man who ever lived. We might expect that if he had unbelieving women in his life, he would have been a good influence on them, right? Surely he would have led them to the Lord and not vice versa. But listen to the tragic consequences of Solomon's relationships with unbelieving women: "For when Solomon was old his wives turned away his heart after other gods, and his heart was not wholly true to the LORD his God" (1 Kings 11:4). If wise King Solomon was ruined by relationships with unbelievers, who do we think we are imagining we can handle it?

This may seem restrictive, but let's face it: As Christians, we'll enjoy our relationships more if we can connect spiritually with our significant other, especially because our faith in Christ is the center of who we are as people. My favorite part of my relationship with my wife, Kim, is that we both love Christ and share His values. We love Him more than each other, and that enhances our love. Our relationship with the Savior brings us closer to one another. It gives us a common bond that nothing else could.

5. The Cultivation Principle

Dating relationships need cultivating. But how do you actually do that? First, you can cultivate your dating relationship best when you see each other first as spiritual siblings. If you apply the Common Ground Principle, you should be interested only in a brother or sister in the Lord. As such, this person is your spiritual sibling before they are a romantic option.

Also, there is safety in numbers. Getting to know a person of the opposite sex is done best in groups at first. Parents, church leaders, and spiritually mature friends should be in the mix (see the Confirmation Principle). This allows a good view into a person's character and personality. But there are limits to what you can discover and evaluate in this context. There is value in time alone, too.

First, let me define "alone." This does not mean that no one else is around. You can eat out together, talk at a coffee shop, go to church, and so forth—these situations provide great opportunities to be alone. In other words, you're interacting only with each other, but you're in a public place. Spending time together with no one else around is asking for trouble. The biggest danger in being alone is the temptation to express inappropriate physical affection (see the Chastity Principle) and inappropriate emotional affection. The place where many get into trouble is in what I call the all-or-nothing category. What I mean by this is that a romance is started with both knowing little about the other person. They go from nothing to a lot very fast. And then if they break up, they go from a lot right back to nothing. This kind of "all or nothingness" can lay the foundation for future problems and even divorce. How? A pattern begins to emerge that if the relationship is not working, the solution is to bail out.

Nothing could be farther from the ideal when it comes to Christians who are pursuing each other. I am not suggesting that you necessarily have to marry the first person you date. We need to be reminded that Christians share a relationship that transcends the arena of romance — that of being spiritual siblings to one another. If you want to cultivate the right kind of relationship, you have to understand this.

Christians are spiritually related to every other believer in the world; they are brothers and sisters. Just as parents set rules and standards for their children's interaction, God has set rules and standards for His children to follow. This weighed heavily on the mind of Christ in the final days of His earthly ministry (see John 13:34-35; 15:12,17). He wanted us to honor each other as spiritual siblings.

The phrase "one another" is a favorite in the Bible to describe the familial relationship that believers share in Christ. There are almost forty commands in the New Testament about believers relating to one another. Romans 12:10 is the fountainhead for all "one anothers": "Love one another with brotherly affection." This love is the commitment to do what is best for the other. If Christian couples apply this kind of selflessness, physical and emotional temptations will be held in check.

6. The Complementarian Principle

John Piper observes,

> The tendency today is to stress the equality of men and women by minimizing the unique significance of our maleness and femaleness. But this depreciation of male and female personhood is a great loss. It is taking a tremendous toll on generations of young men and women who do not know what it means to be a man or a woman.[9]

Contemporary evangelicalism is in the throes of a debate about masculinity and femininity. This is especially evident in the context of preparing for marriage. God has designed men and women to enjoy different roles in marriage. People who disagree with that are called egalitarians. They believe that men's and women's roles in marriage are equal. I disagree, and here's why.

The term *complementarity* comes from the biblical teaching that men and women have been given different roles so they might *complement* each other. The complementarian position recognizes the uniqueness in God's creative order with respect to men and women:

> At the heart of mature masculinity is a sense of benevolent responsibility to lead, provide for, and protect women in ways appropriate to a man's differing relationships. . . .
>
> At the heart of true femininity is a freeing disposition to affirm, receive, and nurture strength and leadership from worthy men in ways appropriate to a woman's differing relationships.[10]

The biblical data are undeniable for these statements (see Genesis 1–3; Ephesians 5:21-33; Colossians 3:18-19; 1 Timothy 3:4,12; Titus 2:3-5; 1 Peter 3:1-7). For men and women to be ready for marriage, they must prepare themselves for these roles. Men need to learn to lead with grace. Their leadership is to be as understanding and trustworthy as that of Jesus Himself (see Ephesians 5:22-33). Following the example of Christ, this leadership is not to be heavy-handed or authoritarian. It should be tender and understanding (see 1 Peter 3:7).

To prepare themselves for marriage, women need to learn wise submission to men worthy of this privilege. This is first learned by submitting to their fathers, church leaders, and other authorities in life. But the Bible does not call a woman to submit to a man in a romantic relationship until she is his wife. The process of learning to submit herself to a man in this way—and discerning whether that man is worthy of such submission—should take place during the dating period.

I believe God's Word clearly teaches a complementarian design for men's and women's roles that flows out of our understanding of masculinity and femininity. Understanding and developing these roles is an important part of preparing for marriage.

This means that a man should be the initiator in a relationship. Because a wife's role is clearly to follow the leadership of her husband, a single woman should allow a man to pursue her only if he is worthy of her submission.

What Do You Think?	Are you an egalitarian or a complementarian? How do you think this affects your dating relationships?

But let's press the issue a bit by looking at our third scenario.

Denise just turned thirty. She is a business professional working in a metropolitan area across the country from her parents. She is active in her local church and busy with friends and activities but has not had any real experience with romantic relationships. She feels her biological clock ticking and wants to get married and have children. What should she do?

Ideally, Denise would not have a job away from the care and protection of her parents, especially because she's a single woman. If for some reason she cannot move back to their area, she should first express her desires to God in prayer. Consideration should be given to whether being a wife and mother is becoming an idol in her heart. And if she wants to be found by the right kind of guy, she should focus her time on serving the body of Christ.

First Corinthians 7 gives wonderful hope for Denise to use her singleness with undivided devotion to Christ (see verse 35) and unhindered ministry for His purposes (see verse 32). Should she move to another church with more single men or even seek to be matched up on a Christian Internet dating service? These questions should be considered with great care and counsel. Speaking with her parents and pastor(s) may provide specific direction. She would be unwise to make such serious decisions without parental and pastoral oversight.

If a single woman such as Denise is attracted to a godly man, but he has not pursued her, it is not her place to be the initiator. She should lay her desires before the Lord and allow Him to direct the man's heart. And disclosing her interest to friends mutual to the man is not necessarily out of line. But if Christian men would learn how to be Christian *men*, I think situations like Denise's would decrease.

7. The Companionship Principle

God invented marriage because man was alone, not because he was lonely. From the very beginning, God has intended relationships to be about glorifying Him by purposeful companionship. So the purpose of marriage is simple: to serve, represent, and glorify God as a two-in-one team. Dating serves as an arena for testing a relationship to see if it glorifies God enough to warrant marriage. This is the Companionship Principle.

One can use dating as the testing ground for marriage only if one understands marriage. That being true, let's go back to the purpose of marriage. The question that must be asked, then, is this: Does the relationship move you to serve, represent, and glorify God better or worse than you could alone?

The best way to find this out is through time — a lot of time. Usually, it's important to go slowly. Take as much time as you need to really get to know a person before you decide that he or she is "the one." On the other hand, going too slowly can make sexual temptation unbearable. Seek the Lord fervently during this time as you're figuring out whether you should marry this person.

Observe your beau in as many contexts as possible. A man should not judge a woman solely on how she looks without makeup; in the same way, a woman should not consider only whether or not a man has good hygiene. Instead, both should determine if the other has a true heart for the things of God.

Though the ability to serve and glorify God together is of utmost importance, it is also legitimate to ask the question, What about physical attraction? Does it play any part in the decision process? The Song of Solomon clearly — and graphically — illustrates that physical attraction is a part of God's design in marital romance (see 4:1-7; 6:4–7:10). This is a divine gift. Notice that Solomon and his bride were physically attracted to each other before they married (see 1:10,15-16; 2:13-14).

Physical attraction should play a part of premarital attraction, but only a part. When Solomon taught his sons about marital satisfaction, he said,

> Let your fountain be blessed,
>> and rejoice in the wife of your youth,
>> a lovely deer, a graceful doe.
> Let her breasts fill you at all times with delight;
>> be intoxicated always *in her love.*
>> (Proverbs 5:18-19, emphasis added)

In other words, physical desire should be satisfied in marriage, but the satisfaction of companionship is more important. And it's amazing how attractive people of godly character can be.

In order to accurately assess a relationship, a thorough understanding of God's design for marriage is crucial. As you consider marriage, it might be a good idea to read more books about marriage than about dating and courting (except this one, of course!).[11]

8. *The Commitment Principle*

One of the most generic phrases in the English language is "I love you." Love is said to be a feeling unlike anything you have ever felt before. Others say love is like a hole in the ground—you fall into it.

If you want to experience biblical love, you need to have the faithfulness and responsibility to love as God loves. The New Testament term for this kind of love is *agape*. It simply means an unconditional commitment to an imperfect person. Ephesians 5:22-33 describes this as the kind of love a married couple should have. It is not based on emotion, selfish gain, or even attraction. (Note: I am not saying that you should not be attracted to the person you marry!)

But what is the nature of such love? God didn't leave us to our own thinking and hormones to decide. *Agape* love is the kind of love God has (see John 3:16), and we have been given a very detailed description of it:

> Love is patient and kind; love does not envy or boast; it is not arrogant or rude. It does not insist on its own way; it is not irritable or resentful; it does not rejoice at wrongdoing, but rejoices with the truth. Love bears all things, believes all things, hopes all things, endures all things. Love never ends. (1 Corinthians 13:4-8)

Love is a commitment. It is a decision to be made and a promise to be kept. It is the way Christians care for one another. And it is the way a husband and wife reflect the glory of Jesus Christ. Real, genuine, sincere, biblical love endures all things and stays committed to an imperfect person. I am not suggesting that you can never break off a dating relationship—even if you have told someone you love him or her. Rather, in a romantic context, those words should be reserved for communicating a permanent relational commitment.

9. *The Communication Principle*

At the core of every problem in marriage and premarital relationships is prideful selfishness. And nothing solves this problem more than communication. If you want to be successful relationally, learning to communicate biblically is nonnegotiable.

Ephesians 4:25-29 teaches that appropriate, godly communication has at least four elements. Paul encouraged the Ephesian believers to communicate verbally (see verse 25), honestly (see verse 25), regularly (see verse 26), and purposefully (see verse 29). Any relationship, romantic or otherwise, would profit from these principles.

One of the most important skills to evaluate and work on in a dating relationship is communication. Jesus said that a person's heart is revealed by what he or she says (see Luke 6:45). God-honoring communication is the bridge that will take you to relational enjoyment and get you over the inevitable conflicts of relationships.

Men and women communicate differently. Learning to clearly say what you mean and to hear what is really being said is more of an art than a science. But there is a key: humility. If you really want to be a better communicator and listener, put the focus of your communication on the other person. Use wisdom in talking about yourself. Beware of the person who likes to talk only about himself or herself. And especially pay attention to how much that person speaks about things in relation to the gospel.

It's simple. We talk about what is important to us. So let Jesus flavor what you say and how you say it. And listen carefully for the sounds of the Savior when you listen to that person you are interested in.

10. The Chastity Principle

One question I am regularly asked by people in romantic relationships is, "How far can we go physically?" The problem is that this question is fundamentally wrong. Another way of phrasing it is, "How close can we get to sin without getting into trouble?" The Chastity Principle involves asking another question altogether: "How holy can we be?"

Physical affection is a privilege of the marriage commitment. Said another way, sex is God's wedding gift, and He doesn't want the present touched until after the wedding! So what does that mean? What about holding hands, hugging, kissing, and so on? Two important texts need our attention:

> Flee from sexual immorality. Every other sin a person commits is outside the body, but the sexually immoral person sins against his own body. Or do you not know that your body is a temple of the Holy Spirit within you, whom you have from God? You are not your own, for you were bought with a price. So glorify God in your body. (1 Corinthians 6:18-20)

> For this is the will of God, your sanctification: that you abstain from sexual immorality. (1 Thessalonians 4:3)

From these two passages, God's counsel about physical affection can be discerned. Sexual sin is prohibited, uniquely offensive to God, damaging, against God's will, a violation of the Holy Spirit's presence, and a sinful use of your body that was bought by the blood of Jesus.

These passages raise another issue that must be tackled: What does it mean to defraud a person in a relationship? First Thessalonians 4:3-7 is a warning against sexual sin. Paul says that immorality is against God's will (see verse 3), a lack of self-control (see verse 4), characteristic of an unredeemed life (see verse 5), sin against a brother (see verse 6), and a lightning rod for God's personal vengeance (see verse 6).

Verse 6 says that to commit sexual sin is to "transgress and wrong his brother in this matter." Some translations use the word *defraud* for the word *wrong* (KJV, NASB). The word translated *defraud* (*pleonektein*) means "to take advantage of," "to claim more," or "to have more than one's due."[12] Note that the object of the verb is "his brother."

Some people use this verse to encourage singles not to defraud each other by sexual sin. Sexual sin is certainly taking advantage of another. However, the verse is better understood as referring to a future spouse who would be violated by a couple's sin. Leon Morris explains, "Promiscuity before marriage refers to the robbing of the other of that virginity which ought to be brought to a marriage. The future partner of such a one has been defrauded."[13]

These verses are also used to prohibit emotional defraud of a person being dated. Care should certainly be given to avoid violating a person in a relationship (see Romans 12:10), but the point of this passage is to show love and respect to a future spouse. In other words, you should treat a person you are dating as if they might become someone else's spouse. How? By being physically pure. It is far better to hurt the feelings of the person you are dating because of a lack of physical affection than to defraud a future spouse.

So what constitutes sexual sin? Jesus said even the fantasy of extramarital or premarital sexual intimacy is sin (see Matthew 5:27-30). Paul went so far as to say that we should not even allow ourselves to be in a situation where lust can be fueled (see Romans 13:14). So how much physical intimacy should an unmarried couple experience? Slim to none. I can hear what you are saying as you read this: "Come on, Rick, be realistic. Nobody can be that puritanical." But listen to the logic of that kind of thinking. Are we really willing to say that the power of our fleshly lust is greater than the power of the Holy Spirit? Purity is possible where there is a desire and willingness to be pure.

Ask yourself if being physical is *necessary*. And by the way, if the person you are dating is putting pressure on you to do more or go farther, you might want to reevaluate if you're with the right person.

First Corinthians 7 contains the most concentrated instruction in the New Testament regarding being single and being married. There are several critical verses in this chapter that need comment: "Now concerning the matters about which you wrote: 'It is good for a man not to have sexual relations with a woman.' But because of the temptation to sexual immorality, each man should have his own wife and each woman her own husband" (verses 1-2).

There is considerable scholarly evidence that the sentence "It is good for a man not to have sexual relations with a woman" is a quotation from a letter the Corinthians had sent Paul.[14] They were asking him if he thought it was a good idea for a married couple to abstain from sex. The following verse contains Paul's answer: If sex is withheld in marriage, immorality could result from temptation. Though many use this verse to teach that "it is good for a man not to touch a woman" (KJV, NASB) before marriage, the context of the phrase does not allow such interpretation. I do, however, think that the principle of abstinence is taught other places in Scripture (see 1 Thessalonians 4:3-7).

This principle is explained later in the chapter (see verses 25-40)—namely that singleness has considerable advantages over marriage. However, if sexual desire is a struggle, then marriage is the God-given way to satisfy these God-given desires. Paul taught that both singleness and marriage are good.

The apostle did not, however, teach that a single person does not have to be self-controlled (see Galatians 5:22-23), nor did he teach that sex is the main reason to get married. He simply urged people to make sure the decision about whether or not to marry is made with godly wisdom. Because 1 Corinthians is an answer to questions the Corinthians sent Paul, he was dealing with specifics unknown to us. But through his answers, the Holy Spirit has provided critical instruction for the church.

SO NOW WHAT?

We live in a world stained by sin. No relationship system can undo the personal and cultural consequences of our depravity. The only hope for us is in the death of Jesus Christ and the gift of His righteousness.

This guided approach to relationships will be practiced by sinful men and women. Thus, it is easy to be extreme on some points and thereby fall into legalism or to be too relaxed on other points, which results in lawlessness. Because my view is less structured than some of the others, a great degree of maturity is required on the part of the couple. Perhaps the biggest danger in this approach is the possibility of making relationships into a simple checklist or a series of hoops to jump through. However, if the Confirmation Principle is used with the right people, most of those mistakes can be avoided.

Two questions I am asked repeatedly as a pastor are, "Does God have a specific will for a believer's life with regard to a mate?" and, "Is there a 'right one' I am supposed to find?"

Yes. But you can't be absolutely sure until you are married! The simple principle is that you choose whom to love and then you love whom you chose. And more important than finding the right person is being the right person.

CONCLUSION

I believe that honoring these biblical principles is more important than whether you date or court. In fact, they ought to be followed regardless of the system a Christian couple uses. It is possible to have a God-honoring dating relationship if these standards are kept. And anyone who is committed to courtship should not disregard them. Even a betrothal model should include them within its strict guidelines. Again, if we are the men and women God calls us to be and God's Word is honored in these ten ways, the process we use is secondary.

The time to begin to apply these principles is not when you find yourself attracted to someone. The time is now! Let me say it one more time: God is more concerned that you are the right kind of person than whether you are using the "right" system. Be who He has called you to be and trust that He will honor your passion for Him as well as your desire for a relationship.

No dating system is perfect. But we should still strive to honor God in how we find a spouse. I find it interesting that when I read Christian biographies, how Christian couples got together is rarely emphasized. Their examples teach us that personal godliness—not dating, courtship, or betrothal—is what made their marriages what they were.

The same is true of us. How we respond to the gospel is the primary factor in making us who we are and in guiding how we navigate the road to marriage. The importance of having a biblical plan for relationships cannot be overstated. My prayer is that this book will cause you to evaluate your thinking and become more Christlike as a result. May God grant you His wisdom in your relationships and the satisfaction found only in salvation through Jesus Christ.

THE GUIDED PATH: AN OVERVIEW

Definition

Guided dating is defined by ten principles that can guide your decision making in your dating relationships. These principles seek to honor Scripture, though there is not one biblically defined way to meet and marry the love of your life.

Distinctives

- Adhering to one particular method, such as courtship or casual dating, can be dangerous because you can become more interested in the rules than in the principles.

- Dating is perfectly acceptable but is not to be done casually.

- Christians should carefully seek guidance from the Word, parents, friends, and other Christian influences to receive confirmation that going forward with a dating relationship is a good idea.

- Honoring the ten principles is more important than whether you date or court—the principles are applicable for any relationship regardless of the method used.

- God is more concerned that you are the right kind of person than whether you are using the "right" system.

Key Verses

- 2 Peter 1:3

- Titus 2:2-8

- Proverbs 12:15

- Philippians 4:10-13

- Romans 12:10

Key Benefits

- Not choosing one particular method for dating can give you freedom in your choices and also encourage you to focus on the person you are rather than the practice you choose.

- With less structure in this approach, you have to be mature about your dating decisions. Dating is a great opportunity to flex your maturity muscles.

- These principles will help you become a better person, whether you're interested in someone right now or not. They will prepare you for a time when you are interested in someone.

- The guided approach is realistic and relevant to today's culture of singles.

Potential Problems

- Perhaps the biggest danger in this approach is the possibility of making relationships into a simple checklist or a series of hoops to jump through.

- Just as with any other approach to dating, there is the potential to become legalistic in following the rules and forget about following the Spirit.

- As the benefits state, maturity is a key element to this approach. Ask God to continue to develop your relationship with Him in order to make wise dating decisions.

THE BETROTHAL PATH | 4

Jonathan Lindvall

JESUS IS GETTING MARRIED. HE LOVES HIS BRIDE AND EAGERLY WAITS for the wedding. He is betrothed.

The church is revealed in Scripture as the bride of Christ. What is our relationship with Jesus? Are we already married? No, the wedding is still in the future. The "marriage supper of the Lamb" (Revelation 19:9)[1] is something we look forward to. So is Christ dating the church right now? Or is He courting us? Perhaps we're engaged to marry Jesus.

No. The church is already in a covenant relationship with our heavenly Bridegroom, even though the wedding is still to come. God created marriage at least partly to reflect His own desire for His relationship with His bride. Our romances are supposed to parallel and reveal the relationship between Christ and the church.

I would like to demonstrate that the scriptural practice described as betrothal (some Bible translations call it espousal) is a universal principle transcending cultures throughout human history and intended by God to provide a romantic and effective transition from singleness to marriage. More important, though, I hope to demonstrate that God ordained betrothal and marriage to reveal something about His heart that no other metaphor reveals. By neglecting God's design, we've lost the picture He wanted to use to reveal His heart for us.

WHAT IS BETROTHAL?

From Scripture, it is clear that biblical betrothal is a covenant relationship that defines the process between singleness and marriage. The covenant is as irrevocable as marriage (no breaking up), but it does not authorize sexual union. The betrothal period is a season of preparation for marriage — particularly for preparing one's heart.

From this understanding, I will argue that betrothal is intended to be the time when a bride and groom begin to draw one another's hearts and release their hearts to each other. It is a foundational season that will color their marital romance permanently. However, before betrothal, any emotional intimacy is inappropriate experimental romance. So in following this approach, the decision of whom to marry is not made on the basis of emotional attraction but rather on some other basis.

God is a romantic. I have always been fascinated by the topic of romance. I have found that most people are similarly drawn to this subject. Apparently God placed this inclination within us right from the beginning. Have you ever noticed that the Bible begins with a wedding? It also ends with a wedding. And the history of mankind has been a continuous unfolding of an incredible love story.

OUR MARRIAGE TO CHRIST

Our own marriages are supposed to be a picture of Christ and His church. In Ephesians 5:22-33, Paul uses what we know of Christ and the church to admonish wives and husbands to relate to one another as God designed. But then he turns the tables and tells us that our marriages, when properly ordered, are actually a picture of Jesus' romance. He says, "This is a great mystery, but I speak concerning Christ and the church" (Ephesians 5:32).

If our marriages are supposed to reveal something of the glorious picture of Christ and the church, that makes it all the more critical that we not mess up the picture. If a culture wanted to redefine marriage in some way, would God be grieved? Marriage isn't solely — or perhaps even primarily — about us. It is about something God has always been trying to reveal about His own desire.

Similarly, what if some culture redefined betrothal? As we know, ours has! Betrothal was an integral part of the pattern of marriage — particularly the relationship of Christ and His bride — throughout both the Old and New Testaments.[2] But it has been cast aside in modern individualistic culture, and even Christians use the argument that it is a cultural novelty unnecessary as a universal principle. I believe we neglect the picture of betrothal to our own harm.

A FAMILIAR STORY

Perhaps the most familiar betrothal story in the Bible occurred with the birth of the Lord Jesus Himself. His mother, Mary, was not yet married when she was "found with child" (Matthew 1:18). At the time, she was "betrothed to Joseph, before they came together" (1:18). When Joseph learned that Mary was pregnant, he was understandably upset. He knew he wasn't the father of the child and so assumed Mary had fallen into immorality. He wanted to call off the wedding.

But Joseph couldn't just call off the wedding as easily as we do in modern society. Today, if a couple is engaged to be married, either party can change his or her mind and call off the marriage at any point prior to the wedding. Thus, until the moment they are recognized as fully married, their relationship is still experimental. (And increasingly, with the ease of no-fault divorce, many even consider marriage experimental.)

But in the Bible, both marriage and betrothal were irrevocable without a scripturally based divorce. Joseph couldn't just change his mind and walk away. He would have had to actually divorce Mary on scriptural grounds in order to revoke the betrothal covenant, although they were not yet married.

We read that Joseph was contemplating a quiet divorce when the Lord intervened by sending an angel saying, "Joseph, son of David, do not be afraid to take to you Mary your wife, for that which is conceived in her is of the Holy Spirit" (Matthew 1:20). In other words, "You have no grounds for the divorce because Mary has not been immoral. Proceed with the marriage."

Note that in the birth narratives of the Lord in both Matthew 1 and Luke 2, Joseph and Mary are clearly stated to be betrothed. Yet they are also referred to as husband and wife despite not yet being married. (This is also seen in Deuteronomy 22:24.) How can this be? Just as Christ and the church are not yet married but are already in a covenant relationship, so a betrothed couple is in a covenant relationship, though they are not yet authorized to be one flesh. We can already be confident in our position as the bride of Christ because our relationship with Him is not probationary or experimental.

What Do You Think?	Did you know that Scripture calls Mary "wife" even though she was unmarried? How does that affect your thinking about dating, betrothal, or engagement?

Betrothal was clearly practiced in both the Old and New Testaments. But just because something was practiced in the biblical culture doesn't mean we are required to practice the same thing. In those days, everyone, even the men, wore robes. Must I wear a robe to be biblical? I don't think so. With this mindset, some argue that the biblical practice of betrothal was simply a cultural phenomenon that was permitted by God. But it's important to recognize that in Scripture, some things are not only described but also prescribed. In some cases, the prescription is given in the form of a command. In others, it is clearly assumed in the definitions. Some might argue that the Scriptures never directly forbid an unmarried couple to engage in premarital intimacy. Yet the clear definition of fornication and the statements in Scripture condemning it make it abundantly clear that sexual intimacy prior to marriage is not permitted.

Scripture provides similar clarity regarding betrothal. There is strong evidence that betrothal is a universal principle for mankind that comes from God. This betrothal principle is the same for all cultures throughout history, just as the principle of marriage is universal and not culturally relative.

I do want to note here that we are not under law but under grace. Paul said in Galatians 5:18, "But if you are led by the Spirit, you are not under the law." We are neither under the Old Covenant law nor some New Testament set of rules. Jesus "wiped out the handwriting of requirements that was against us, which was contrary to us. And He has taken it out of the way, having nailed it to the cross" (Colossians 2:14). That said, we are still to love the law (see Psalm 119:97,113,163,165) and allow it to shape our frame of reference, although we are not under it.

Some have argued that applying betrothal to modern culture is legalism and bondage. Yet these same people generally uphold the principle of marriage as binding on all people. Similarly, Scripture reveals betrothal to be another universal principle in God's heart.

Let's consider some evidence of this. One of the strongest evidences I know of is God's prescription of the penalties for sexual immorality. In

Deuteronomy 22:22-29 God dealt with this question. He said, "If a man is found lying with a woman married to a husband, then both of them shall die—the man that lay with the woman, and the woman; so you shall put away the evil from Israel" (verse 22).

If a man committed sexual immorality with a married woman, it was called adultery. They were violating the marriage covenant, and God's penalty for their violation was death (see Leviticus 20:10). God didn't require this simply because marriage was a cultural practice He condoned within the Jewish society. He defined and imposed marriage as a sacred institution within which was the only permissible expression of physical intimacy. And He revealed His loathing of violations of the marriage covenant so strongly that He required capital punishment for them.

But is the penalty the same if, for example, a couple of young single people are found to have been physically intimate with one another? No. Although it is still sin, the penalty is different. Deuteronomy 22:28-29 says, "If a man finds a young woman who is a virgin, who is not betrothed, and he seizes her and lies with her, and they are found out, then the man who lay with her shall give to the young woman's father fifty shekels of silver, and she shall be his wife because he has humbled her; he shall not be permitted to divorce her all his days."

That's a bit shocking. If a couple of teenagers fall into sin together, what is the penalty? They just have to get married (and they are never permitted to divorce).[3] Why is the case of the single virgin different from that of the married woman? The key lies in the primary difference between adultery and fornication. They both involve the same physical act, but adultery includes the violation of a covenant; if at least one of the parties is married, what would otherwise have been fornication is instead classified as adultery.

God specified that the penalty for adultery was death, but the penalty for fornication was not so extreme. It may seem like a double standard because in both cases, the physical act is identical. But adultery is dealt with more harshly because God sees the violation of covenants as a very serious matter.

Notice that so far, the discussion of immorality with a virgin specifically relates to a virgin who is not betrothed. But what about a virgin who *is* betrothed?

Between the discussion of the married woman and the single virgin in Deuteronomy 22, God introduces a third marital state. Today, we think of someone as either married or single. But God recognizes a third category: Those who are betrothed are neither single nor yet married. So what happens if a betrothed virgin is immoral? In God's eyes, is it adultery or fornication?

In verses 23-24, God says, "If a young woman who is a virgin is betrothed to a husband, and a man finds her in the city and lies with her, then you shall bring them both out to the gate of that city, and you shall stone them to death with stones, the young woman because she did not cry out in the city, and the man because he humbled his neighbor's wife; so you shall put away the evil from among you."

God apparently sees the immorality of a betrothed person as adultery and required execution. One might ask, "How could this be adultery as there is not yet a covenant? They're not married yet." This presupposes our modern understanding that the covenant begins at the wedding. But God recognizes the covenant when two people commit to a future marriage, not just when a marriage certificate is signed. We will evaluate some common assumptions and practices in light of this truth a little later.

While I find this technical discussion persuasive, there is evidence that I find even more compelling. I introduced this initially and have returned to it several times. But let me reiterate it one more time. Is the church already married to Christ? No, the wedding is still in the future. Are we dating Christ? Is He simply playing with our emotions or checking us out to see if He really wants us? No. He has already chosen us, not based on our merit or compatibility with Him but because He simply wants us.

So if we're not married to Christ yet and we're not dating Him, what are we? Are we courting Christ? As superior to dating as courtship is, it is still experimental. Jesus isn't just seriously checking us out. Well, then, we must be engaged to Christ, right? That depends on how one defines engagement. By today's definition of engagement, the answer would be no; we are not in a relationship in which we are optimistic but unsure that we will ultimately be with Him for eternity. Jesus can't call off the wedding—His relationship with us is covenantal; He can't break the bond because He can't violate His own character.

Paul says in 2 Corinthians 11:2, "For I am jealous for you with godly jealousy. For I have *betrothed* you to one husband, that I may present you as a chaste virgin to Christ" (emphasis added). The church is betrothed to Jesus! We will never understand our relationship to Him as fully as He desires until we recover *in our practice of premarital relationships* the picture He ordained to portray our current relationship with Himself.

What Do You Think?	Jonathan says he finds the discussion on sexual purity persuasive toward his argument for betrothal but the discussion on Christ's church even more persuasive. Which do you find more persuasive, if either? Why?

MODERN-DAY APPLICATION

So what does all this mean in practice? How do we apply it? In recent generations, we have lost the heritage of betrothal. How can it be recovered for the glory of God? There are certain practices we must begin implementing for the picture to be accurate. And there are other practices that we need to avoid to keep the picture from being skewed or corrupted. Let's consider the practical side of all this.

First, we must stay sexually pure. Paul instructed "that no man go beyond and defraud his brother" (1 Thessalonians 4:6, KJV) regarding the matter of moral purity. The Greek word translated "go beyond" is *huperbaino*, meaning literally to "cross the line." Although we may not all agree on where the line is, it is clear there is a line we are not to cross, and that is what defines physical purity.

But as important as physical purity is, it is not the only issue. There were two things Paul admonished avoiding. The second is defrauding. What is that? Defrauding is causing another person to expect something desirable and then neglecting to fulfill the implied promise. When a business makes advertising claims that are exaggerated, customers feel defrauded when they realize they have been tricked. Parents often defraud their children by making promises they don't fulfill. Does defrauding ever happen in romantic relationships? Certainly. In fact, the assumption in our culture is that this is what makes romance romantic. For some, the risk of being jilted may even make the game seem that much more adventurous.

As I ponder Paul's admonition, it occurs to me that the best contemporary term for what he warned against is *flirting*. Flirting is the act of trying to draw someone's interest knowing that any interest generated will not likely be fulfilled.

Western culture finds flirting so acceptable that we easily confuse it with basic friendliness. In fact, refusing to flirt or respond to flirtation is often seen as rudeness. If a woman seems uncomfortable with special attention from a man, she is seen as prudish. If a man seems to resist responding to "good-natured" teasing from a woman, it may cause people to assume he is chauvinistic. We've been conditioned to see subtle flirtation as innocent fun, but the Bible says it is wrong.

Paul uses an interesting Greek term in his admonition to women in 1 Timothy 2:9. *The King James Version* rendition particularly arouses curiosity. Paul said women should "adorn themselves . . . with shamefacedness." What in the world is shamefacedness? In Noah Webster's original dictionary, he defined it as "excessive modesty."[4] The term *excessive* would seem to imply something we should avoid, yet Scripture commands women (and I think men should practice this, too) to "adorn themselves" with this excessive modesty. More contemporary Bible translations use words such as *propriety* or a form of *discreet*. The Greek word Paul used is *aidos*. The etymological roots of the word imply "downcast eyes." He seems to be encouraging the avoidance of overt eye contact!

This may truly seem excessive to the modern mind. But at the very least, Paul is cautioning against forwardness. Very frequently what one intends only as courteous flirtation is misinterpreted as romantic interest. I have talked to numerous young people who claim they are simply being friendly but are leaving a wake of misunderstanding behind them with people who misinterpret their friendliness as romantic invitations.

To clarify this point, I sometimes ask a young single person if it would be proper for me to be friends with his or her mother. Usually the initial answer is that this is obviously acceptable. But as I press the matter and ask if I, without my wife's involvement, could be friends with some other married woman without also being friends with her husband, most Christian young people acknowledge that there is something questionable in the thought.

I can be cordial and cautiously friendly with women other than my wife, but there is a certain unspoken limitation that I must maintain in all my relationships with other women. I can tease my wife in ways that would be inappropriate with any other woman. It is clearly wrong for me to flirt with other women. I am to be faithful to my wife both physically and emotionally.

If this emotional purity and cautiousness is required of married people, might it not also be required of single people? I believe so. My sons and daughters need to be just as cautious as I do in their friendliness toward those of the opposite gender. Otherwise they are not being shamefaced and risk drawing someone's interest without the ability or even intention of fulfilling it. Whether intentional or not, flirting is defrauding. And dating is simply a modern cultural structure to facilitate flirting. Imagine going on a date with someone who refused to flirt. Such a platonic interaction would be hard to classify as a date at all.

What Do You Think?	Jonathan says flirting is a form of defrauding. Have you had any experiences that cause you to agree? Disagree? If you agree, what are some ways you can show appropriate friendliness without flirting?

Paul made it clear that single people should not be distracted by romance. He said in 1 Corinthians 7:32-33, "But I want you to be without care. He who is unmarried cares for the things of the Lord—how he may please the Lord. But he who is married cares about the things of the world—how he may please his wife." In modern Christian circles, we have reversed this. We think that single youth need to actively pursue romantic relationships and then, once they are married, settle down and focus on the Lord. In contrast, Paul says that singles are to focus on the Lord; they are to focus on romance only after they are married (or presumably, betrothed).

SO HOW DOES ONE ACTUALLY BECOME BETROTHED?

I often am interviewed on Christian radio stations before putting on my seminars. When the interviewers realize I will be speaking against dating, they typically convey their shock with a question such as, "How would people ever marry if they don't date?" But dating is a recent invention. Historically, its rise is linked to the advent and widespread use of the automobile in the early 1900s. Dating has been practiced (and assumed) for enough generations now that few bother to question it. In fact, in our society, assumptions of the normalcy of dating are so deeply ingrained that we can't imagine how someone could get married without the dating process.

So how do you enter a betrothal relationship? The first things you should do are (1) commit yourself to bring pleasure and glory to the Lord Jesus in every aspect of your life, (2) give your heart in honor to your parents (see Proverbs 23:26), and (3) commit to save yourself, both physically and emotionally, for the one you will eventually marry.

Having firmly committed to all these things before the Lord, if you begin to wonder about a particular person as a potential spouse, you should immediately reveal this inclination to your parents. I have asked my own children to come to me at the first sign of finding themselves romantically drawn to someone. When they do, I affirm to them God's wonderful design in making men and women attractive to one another. I remind them of what a joyous thing it will be to be able to present to their future spouse not only undefiled bodies but also hearts that have no regrets of previous entanglements.

Then I help them think through two possibilities. Let's say I'm dealing with my daughter. I help her see that on the one hand, if this *is* the man God eventually wants her to marry, it will be beneficial for him to know that she was careful not to prematurely release her heart to him. It will help him believe that she saved herself entirely for him. It will give both him and her confidence in her self-control, thus helping to avoid later doubts and the temptation to harbor petty jealousies.

On the other hand, if this fellow is *not* the one God eventually wants her to marry, allowing herself to experiment with the pleasure of temporary romance will likely hinder her from later enjoying a lifelong brother-sister relationship with him without embarrassment. (I've been married since 1976, but I still find fellowship with former girlfriends quite awkward because I realize I defrauded them by raising hopes that were not ultimately fulfilled). More subtly, the memories and regrets of an experimental romance with this guy would compromise her joy in being able to offer herself both physically and emotionally whole to her future spouse. And a temporary romantic fling and the inevitable breakup with this man would almost certainly have a negative effect on the rest of the people she fellowships with by fostering gossip, rivalries, mistrust, distraction, and so on.

MY SEARCH FOR BETROTHAL

In 1972 when I was a youth pastor, I was introduced to teaching that encouraged me to involve my parents in my romantic decisions. I found such an idea preposterous. Parents? No way! I couldn't imagine anyone less qualified to advise young people about romance. Parents are past the season of romance, I figured. What would they know about it?

But the speaker didn't simply encourage minor involvement of parents in young people's romantic lives. He argued that we should bring everything, including our love life, under our parents' authority. He contended that if I was interested in dating a particular young lady, I should first seek my parents' blessing. I thought that was the most bizarre thing I had ever heard.

But his ideas got even stranger. He continued that if I succeeded in getting my parents' blessing, I should seek the girl's parents' blessing before even inviting her to go out with me. I could imagine the embarrassment of getting my parents' blessing, getting the girl's parents' blessing, and finally asking the girl, only for her to say, "No."

I thought, *I'm not going through all that! You show me in Scripture where you got such an idea.* Being a youth pastor who had been raised with good Bible teaching all my life, I was confident that such an approach wasn't found in Scripture.

I had been taught that if you ever hear a doctrine that is new, be careful. If it is truly new, it is no doubt a false doctrine. Well, I had never heard such a teaching before, so obviously this one had to be false. So I set out to prove this speaker wrong. I was going to show that he was taking things out of context. I studied every Scripture reference I could find about marriage, weddings, husbands, wives, brides, grooms, and so on. I was going to show that my current dating assumptions were perfectly scriptural. The only problem was that virtually every relevant Scripture I found affirmed this speaker's views of parental authority in the process of selecting a spouse.

Finally, I gave up and admitted he was right. However, as I continued to study, I began to conclude that this man hadn't gone far enough. In fact, dating wasn't in the Bible at all. Although I would now question the process of my logic at the time, I concluded dating must be a sin because it wasn't practiced in the Bible. In my mind, this man was a compromiser!

I wish you could have seen the shocked faces of the young people in my youth group when I announced my conclusion that dating was a sin. In my seminars, I tell the rather humorous story of how I persuaded all of them to give up dating completely. One of the keys was accurately defining dating. We brainstormed together and ultimately all agreed that the most concise definition of dating is "temporary romance."

I helped my youth group recognize that dating implies there will be an end to the romance. That means someone is almost certain to be hurt in the process. Our society has institutionalized what I have come to call "the broken-heart syndrome," assuming it is normal, necessary, and healthy.

I have had people accuse me of simply fleeing pain. They think I must have gone through some traumatic romantic breakup that made me overreact in fear that my own children will experience the same thing. They argue that pain is a part of life and that we should embrace it as God's provision for our maturation.

I'm not recommending a self-focus in which we try to avoid experiencing pain personally. My regrets have little to do with any pain I may have experienced. My greater regret is the pain I inflicted through flirting and dating. I encourage young people to avoid the sin of hurting others.

By God's grace, I persuaded my whole youth group to give up the practice of dating. The only problem was that there had to be some process for moving from singleness to marriage. I knew dating was a historic novelty and was failing miserably. But what should we replace it with?

As I read of practices prior to the advent of dating in the early 1900s, I frequently came across the word *courtship*. I began teaching something I called "biblical courtship." I defined courtship as a romantic relationship between two single people in which (1) they have the full blessing of both sets of parents, (2) they are of marriageable age, and (3) they are seriously considering marrying one another. But beginning in the early 1990s, people began to report that courtship wasn't working. How could courtship not work?

I recall one father who shared that his daughter had given up dating in favor of courtship but was still being defrauded. He told me how she had courted one fellow after another. Now she was in her fourth courtship, and it appeared likely to fail as well.

I protested, "That's not courtship. That's dating." But her father insisted, "No, it's courtship. In each of these romantic relationships, the couple had the full blessing of both sets of parents, they were each of marriageable age, and they were seriously considering one another as marriage partners. But the courtships didn't last, and my daughter has been repeatedly defrauded."

Ouch! I had to admit he was right. His daughter was practicing courtship just as I had taught it. Why didn't it succeed in protecting her from defrauding and being defrauded? Something was missing.

I remember another time someone challenged my teaching on biblical courtship by asking, "Where do we find courtship in the Bible?" I was able to demonstrate the principle of parental authority and protection in Scripture, but does that equate to courtship?

I had to admit that neither the word *courtship* nor even the idea of courtship is ever found in Scripture. Yet people obviously got married in the Bible. How did they select a spouse and move from singleness to marriage?

As I began to honestly search the Scriptures, endeavoring to shed my cultural assumptions, the Lord allowed me to see something obvious that my previous biases had blinded me to. In the Bible, single people got married through the process of betrothal.

As I've said, betrothal is a covenant relationship prior to the marriage itself in which a couple commits to marry one another in the future. Even if they are not "in love" with one another, they enter into a season of preparation for their anticipated marriage.

How did a couple prepare for marriage in the Bible? No doubt the young lady had physical preparations—the equivalent of today's hope chest, perhaps including her wardrobe. We know the young man prepared a home for his bride during the betrothal period.

But I suspect the primary preparation was emotional. While some no doubt had secretly been imagining marrying the one they were now betrothed to, for others, the idea of marrying this particular person was a novelty. And they didn't love one another yet!

FALLING IN LOVE AND THE DIFFERENCE BETWEEN COURTSHIP AND BETROTHAL

Today, we have the notion that emotional bonding—"falling in love"—should precede the commitment to marry. Is it possible we have the order reversed? When should a couple come to love one another? In modern individualistic culture, we are told to "marry the one you love." Most contemporary Christians see romantic love as a prerequisite for marriage. But where do we get such a notion? Does the Bible ever suggest that we should try to figure out whom we love, particularly before deciding whom to marry?

We are constantly being told to "listen to your heart." But our hearts will deceive us. God says,

> The heart is deceitful above all things,
> And desperately wicked. (Jeremiah 17:9)

Modern feel-good counselors advise us to "trust your heart." But Scripture says, "He who trusts in his own heart is a fool" (Proverbs 28:26). Everything in our "If it feels good, do it" culture persuades young people, "Follow your heart." But God's Word exhorts,

> Hear, my son, and be wise;
> And guide your heart in the way. (Proverbs 23:19)

Our emotions are a blessing from God, but our feelings are not to guide us. We are to guide our hearts rather than following them.

The Bible doesn't say, "Marry the one you love" but rather, in essence, "Love the one you marry" (see Ephesians 5:25,28; Colossians 3:19; Titus 2:4). Many will immediately protest, saying that I am proposing unromantic and loveless arranged marriages. Let me put the reader's mind at ease. Imposing arranged marriages on single people is not biblical. And I will demonstrate that. Proverbs 30:21-23 lists four things by which "the earth is perturbed." One of them is "an unloved woman when she gets a husband" (verse 23, NASB).

I don't believe the Scriptures suggest marrying someone you don't love. But neither do I believe the Scriptures encourage experimenting with various romantic partners until you settle on the one you determine to marry. That is the process of defrauding.

What Do You Think?	When Jonathan says, "The Bible doesn't say, 'Marry the one you love' but rather, in essence, 'Love the one you marry,'" how do you react?

What is the difference between betrothal and courtship? The emphasis in courtship is on embracing the protection of parental authority. While I am persuaded the Lord is pleased with that, and I highly encourage incorporating the scriptural principle of parental authority within betrothal, the key to betrothal is commitment, which is missing in courtship. Although I wouldn't recommend it, a couple might conceivably practice the commitment principle of betrothal without the involvement of their parents.

Another way of looking at the distinction between betrothal and courtship is as follows: Courtship allows, or rather encourages, a probationary period of romantic experimentation prior to a commitment, whereas betrothal implies an emotional preparation period following the commitment. Some courtship proponents combine these two, encouraging a courtship period prior to the betrothal. I believe this negates one of the most powerful benefits of betrothal: eliminating romantic experimentation in favor of saving your heart for the one person you are confident you will marry.

However, just as in courtship, you should get your parents' authorization on your relationship. Scripturally, the woman at the very least is to be protected by her parents' authority, although this practice does protect the man as well. In fact, throughout the Bible, marriage is repeatedly defined as a woman being "given in marriage." If a young man and woman give each other a pledge (as in the story of the tailor and Tevya's daughter in *Fiddler on the Roof*), according to Scripture, her father can overrule her on the first day he hears of her vow and "none of her vows nor her agreements by which she has bound herself shall stand; and the LORD will release her, because her father overruled her" (Numbers 30:5). But if "her father holds his peace, then all her vows shall stand" (30:4).

God is very concerned with covenant keeping. He commanded, "If a man makes a vow to the LORD, or swears an oath to bind himself by some agreement, he shall not break his word; he shall do according to all that proceeds out of his mouth" (Numbers 30:2). One of the prerequisites of dwelling in God's presence (see Psalm 15:1) is to be one "who swears to his own hurt and does not change" (15:4). Jesus wants us to be people of our word. He says to "let your 'Yes' be 'Yes,' and your 'No,' 'No'" (Matthew 5:37; James 5:12).

In today's culture, if a couple of young people agree to get married but later change their minds, we find that acceptable. But in the Bible, a betrothed couple could not change their minds. The covenant had already begun. However, there was still a season of preparation allowing them, among other things, to grow in their eager anticipation and let their hearts bond to one another before they actually became one flesh.

Even most modern Christians find this shocking because we have been persuaded (brainwashed?) by the media and other cultural influences that single people should experiment with various romantic partners to determine who they are "compatible with." This same argument is now being used by much of our permissive society to condone and even encourage "safe sex" with various partners to find out whom one would be physically compatible with.

Hopefully God's people recognize this deceit clearly. We know God has given each of us the physical capacity to be compatible with whomever He calls us to marry. We don't need to experiment or test these capacities with various partners to find out whom we physically fit with. Yet we still cling to the notion that we must experiment with many romantic partners to determine our emotional compatibility. This is a novel idea historically. The truth is that God has given us not only the physical capability but also the emotional capacity and personality flexibility to be joyfully compatible with whomever He calls us to marry.

I'm not denying that parents and young people are wise to evaluate prospective marriage partners for godly character, skills, inclinations, and perhaps even pleasing temperament. But ultimately, we have overemphasized this personality compatibility and used it as a rationalization for encouraging single people to yield to fleshly desires (within varying limitations) and exploit one another in experimental relationships.

WHAT WILL YOUR BETROTHAL LOOK LIKE?

If God recognizes the covenant at the betrothal, then is it already essentially marriage? Why should a couple in this situation not be allowed to become one flesh? God distinguishes between betrothal and marriage. They are similar in that betrothal is as binding as marriage and is obviously a step toward marriage. But they are different in that betrothal is a time of preparation for the ultimate union between the husband and wife. In the Bible, what does the wedding authorize? The wedding authorizes the one-flesh union between the husband and wife. Then what does the betrothal authorize?

I believe the betrothal authorizes the couple to begin releasing their hearts to one another. Prior to being betrothed, a young woman who has guarded her heart (in accordance with the instruction in Proverbs 4:23 to "keep your heart with all diligence") has purposed to save not only her body but also her heart for the man she will ultimately marry. She is poised to be a one-man woman both physically and emotionally.

Similarly, I desire that all of my five sons become elders one day. One of the qualifications of this, "husband of one wife" (1 Timothy 3:2,12; Titus 1:6), literally means "man of one woman." Although this undoubtedly refers particularly to physical purity, I want all of them to be one-woman men both physically and emotionally.

Imagine if on our wedding day I had been able to tell Connie, "I have saved myself completely for you, both physically and emotionally. I have never allowed myself to have a romantic relationship with anyone. I have saved my heart, as well as my body, for you." Imagine if she had been able to say the same to me. We both regret our previous romantic relationships that compromised our hearts, though thankfully not our bodies.

Betrothal isn't foolproof. Selfish people practicing betrothal will bend it to their own ends rather than using it as a God-given pattern for their protection and His glory. However, dating, courtship, or any other pattern of romantic experimentation makes defrauding and regrets much more possible—even likely—no matter how well-intentioned the participants are.

APPLICATION

With all this in mind, let me apply these principles to the three fictitious scenarios each contributor to this book has been asked to address.

Scenario 1: Jenny and David, high school juniors in the same church youth group

First, I would encourage David and Jenny to reveal their inclinations to their parents. I would advise their parents to encourage them to guard their hearts against (even unintentionally) drawing the other's interest or releasing their own heart. They should relate to one another as if they were someone else's future spouse: cordially, but with a distant friendliness. (Just as married men and women must be cautious regarding how friendly they are with someone of the opposite gender, so should single people. We all recognize when we think of our own parents, for example, that as a married man, our father can be guardedly friendly with women other than our mother, but he should not have close friendships with women like he can have with other men. And the same goes for our mother.)

Following the ideal betrothal model, David and Jenny should each eagerly look forward to a joyful future marriage without allowing themselves to speculate who their actual spouse will be until they are confident that God is directly leading them to one person through the guidance of their parents.

Scenario 2: Steve and Rachel, college students at a secular university

God uses even ungodly authorities to protect and guide His people. Proverbs 21:1 says,

> The king's heart is in the hand of the LORD,
>   Like the rivers of water;
> He turns it wherever He wishes.

Although none of the parents are believers, Steve and Rachel should expect God to use them in the process of guiding them into a marriage pleasing to Him.

As in the previous scenario, I believe Steve and Rachel should share their growing inclinations with their parents and welcome their counsel or cautions. If Steve begins to express his interest more overtly, Rachel should encourage him to communicate with her parents before proceeding. If any of the parents express reservations about the relationship, Steve and Rachel should entrust it to the Lord, allowing Him to teach them the value of waiting on Him. They should anticipate that if He is the one leading them toward one another, He will change their parents' hearts and confirm His direction through them.

According to the scriptural pattern of betrothal, if Steve is persuaded that Rachel is the one he should marry, he should ask her father's permission to marry her. The covenant in a scriptural betrothal was primarily between the father of the bride (who gives her in marriage) and the groom (who receives her). Yet I believe we do well to be sure all six people (four parents plus the potential groom and bride) are in agreement before entering a covenant.

Once Steve has Rachel's parents' blessing—and hopefully the blessing of his own parents—he is then free to ask Rachel to marry him. If, as in some cases, he is too shy to ask, there is interesting scriptural precedent for the woman's father to initiate the process (see Joshua 15:16; Judges 1:12; 1 Samuel 17:25; 18:20-26). Nor would it be inappropriate to have a friend-matchmaker initiate things. Prior to this, there should be no flirting or romantic experimentation, which would essentially be dabbling with one another's hearts.

If, after much prayer and after confirming that her parents have no objections, Rachel senses Steve's proposal is of the Lord, she would accept it. Steve and Rachel should then make their betrothal publicly known, perhaps announcing it to the church congregation and requesting to be held accountable to fulfill their promise.

During their betrothal, Steve and Rachel should draw toward one another's hearts in eager anticipation of their upcoming wedding. They should use this season as a time for preparation: physically (economically), emotionally, and spiritually. They should expect the Lord to use their betrothal to reveal to them and to others observing them more of His heart for His bride—the church—and His relationship with her as they experience a foreshadowing of the Great Romance the church has and will continue to have with Christ.

Scenario 3: Denise, a thirty-year-old, single business professional

First, Denise should seek the Lord about whether He would like for her to return home to be under the protection of her parents. If a woman is to be "given in marriage" by her father, there is at least a possible hint that she should remain "kept" by him prior to that. It's interesting that even for a man, a literal reading of the phrase "for this reason a man shall leave his father and mother" (Matthew 19:5; Mark 10:7; Ephesians 5:31) may imply that he should stay with his parents until marriage.

Every Christian single needs to yield his or her desire for marriage to the Lord. Although the desire is good and is something God Himself created, all of us must still surrender everything in our lives to the Lord. We can confidently know that it is not normally God's will for people to remain single (see Genesis 2:18), yet we must also be willing to be exceptions and allow the Lord to fulfill our needs and desires through a celibate lifestyle.

But I also believe it would be quite acceptable for a single person like Denise to tell her Christian community that she desires to marry and would be open to introductions. However, I would encourage her to avoid the temptation to lower her standards or compromise her convictions. I would recommend having any prospective suitor interact with her parents and trusted friends first to guard her heart from getting ahead of her. This way both she and the prospective suitor can learn about one another with less emotional vulnerability.

CONCLUSION

Although Connie and I didn't understand the principles of betrothal at the time, by God's grace, our marriage came about in a similar way. The Lord used my parents to show me that I was to marry Connie. Although I was not yet "in love" with her, I obeyed His leading and asked her parents' permission to marry her.

After I proposed to her, it took Connie four months to discern the Lord's will clearly. I repeatedly asked if she had gotten direction from Him, but she wouldn't be swayed. When she finally knew she had heard from the Lord, we were excited, but I don't think we were really in love yet. Instead, it was during our engagement that we fell in love.

My marriage is wonderfully sweet and very romantic. But at its very core, it isn't based on love. It is based on submission to the Lord. The romance is a by-product of our obedience to God.

THE BETROTHAL PATH: AN OVERVIEW

Definition

Betrothal is a covenant relationship that defines the process between singleness and marriage. The covenant is as irrevocable as marriage (no breaking up), but it does not authorize physical union. The betrothal period is a season of preparation for marriage — particularly preparation of your heart.

Distinctives

- Breaking up is unacceptable. Once you are betrothed, marriage is inevitable. Therefore, careful seeking of God's will is necessary. Your parents should be involved in this process, helping you seek God's Word and His leading.

- Human marriage is metaphorical for the church's marriage with Christ. Although our wedding feast with our Bridegroom in heaven has not yet happened, we are betrothed to Him right now, and that covenant cannot be broken.

- Although the covenant is as irrevocable as marriage, sexual union isn't permitted until you are actually married.

- If you date or flirt with someone you are not betrothed to, you are defrauding him or her, his or her future spouse, and your future spouse.

- In betrothal, the motto is not "Marry the one you love" but rather "Love the one you marry."

Key Verses

- 2 Corinthians 11:2; Ephesians 5:22-23; Revelation 19:9 (bride of Christ)

- Matthew 1:18-20

- Deuteronomy 22:22-29

- 1 Corinthians 7:32-33

- 1 Thessalonians 4:6; 1 Timothy 2:9 (defrauding)

Key Benefits

- Betrothal helps protect against emotional and physical damage because you are giving your heart and body solely to one person.

- Unlike dating or courtship, betrothal is prescribed in Scripture. So if you're looking for a way to follow Scripture more explicitly, betrothal is a good option.

- In betrothal, you enter a committed relationship from the get-go, instead of anticipating or being insecure about a breakup.

- "Falling in love" is a by-product of betrothal instead of a requirement for marriage.

- Betrothal, like courtship, creates an environment for obeying God by honoring your parents.

Potential Problems

- You have to be careful when making this crucial decision because "the heart is deceitful above all things" (Jeremiah 17:9). You could make hasty decisions if you're following your heart only and not tapping in to Christ's words and will.

- Betrothal requires that a bride and groom make an effort to set good communication patterns during their betrothal, as they are to have had virtually no intimate conversation prior to the covenant.

- Betrothal could be used as a manipulative tool for selfish people who are not surrendered to Christ. It is a good protection only when practiced by loving people.

THE PURPOSEFUL PATH | 5

Jeramy & Jerusha Clark

JUST OVER FIVE YEARS AGO, WE BEGAN A JOURNEY WITH THIS QUESTION in mind: Is dating an acceptable, God-honoring way of getting to know someone of the opposite sex? Allow us to explain briefly how we came to ask that question in the first place.

Both of us were raised in solid Christian homes. As young adults, our parents allowed us—even encouraged us—to date in healthy ways. At church, pastors and youth leaders spoke about "dating well." Back then, if people were asking whether the institution of dating was inherently flawed, the question certainly didn't come to the forefront.

Only a few years later, the issue was not only front and center, but it also sparked some of the most heated exchanges among Christians.

Every day, we work with single Christians ranging from teens to thirty-somethings—we've led the young-adult ministries at several churches in addition to writing and speaking. In a job that revolves around young believers, as you can imagine, "relationships" is one of the hottest topics. Because of this, we felt called to weigh in on the dating debate. And though we've found that single believers of divergent ages articulate themselves differently, most have similar questions about relating to their male or female counterparts.

After years of observation, we feel strongly that no formula for godly interaction between the sexes exists. There is no "one way" that works for everyone or in every circumstance. We're convinced that for young adults who love the Lord and long to please Him, dating is one option. Not everyone has to date, but single Christians can enjoy appropriate dating relationships if they approach the practice with God's perspective and guidelines.

While we wholeheartedly affirm that many Christians need to rethink their standards, particularly when it comes to emotional and physical promiscuity, we do not feel that a believer needs to reject dating in order to stay focused on God and growing in holiness. Instead, we firmly believe singles can be taught not only how to relate but also how to exercise discernment in dating relationships.

In other words, dating can be an acceptable, God-honoring option for single Christians, provided they apply the foundational truths of Scripture to the specific circumstances of their relationships with the opposite sex.

What Do You Think? | Some of the contributors in this book have mentioned emotional promiscuity as being inappropriate. What do you think emotional promiscuity is? What do you think is a good standard for levels of emotional intimacy in premarital relationships?

Psalm 19:7-8 teaches us,

> The revelation of GOD is whole
> and pulls our lives together.

> The signposts of GOD are clear
> and point out the right road.
> The life-maps of GOD are right,
> showing the way to joy.
> The directions of GOD are plain
> and easy on the eyes. (MSG)

If we truly believe that God's directions are "plain" and His signposts "clear," we can trust that He will guide us and pull all the areas of our lives together.

Because as a couple, we believe that His Word can and will change how people interact with the opposite sex, we've spent the last few years searching the Scriptures as well as speaking with Christian singles and observing them live out their godly convictions.

The following pages will outline what God has taught us. We're going to look first at what dating is; then we'll focus on specific principles that can guide purposeful dating relationships.

A BRIEF NOTE ABOUT HISTORY

People often wonder how and why dating came about. While the scope of this book cannot take into account all the factors that contributed to the rise of dating, it is important to recognize some of the historical and sociological realities that bear on our present-day relationships.

In the past century, men and women were thrown together and required to relate as never before. The rise of public schooling meant boys and girls spent more time in one another's company. As women entered the workforce in greater numbers, they became not merely wives, mothers, and sisters but also colleagues and competitors. Even in churches, men and women began to discuss spiritual ideas in closer contact.

In the past, if men and women got to know one another at all, they did so in private settings, mostly in the home. Today, men and women interact in a primarily public world, learning about one another in all sorts of settings. For many, even for some believers, this world is often disconnected from true community, godly families, and loving homes.

Christians can respond to the social and historical evolution of relationships between the sexes in three ways. They can reject dating outright, trying to take the interaction between men and women back into the private realm of family and home. On the other end of the spectrum, they can wholeheartedly embrace dating as both a social norm and a good way for men and women to get to know one another. Our position lies between these two extremes. We neither believe that people must return to the way men and women interacted a hundred years ago, nor do we claim that Christians should throw caution to the wind and adopt the modern practice of dating.

There's nothing inherently godly about imitating the past, especially when it's entirely impossible to recreate the historical social structure that dictated the ways in which men and women interacted at any given time. Few seem ready to advocate a return to the practices of dowries and arranged marriages in which the bride and groom meet for the first time at the altar, yet these are both customs the Bible describes. We accept that these practices were social constructions of a particular time and place. In applying the principles of God's Word to relationships with the opposite sex, we need not reestablish all the mores of biblical times.

Nor should believers imitate the practices of contemporary culture without deep consideration and discernment. Much of twenty-first-century dating seems to revolve around flirting, "hooking up," and heartbreak. But must it *necessarily* be so? We think not.

As we dated—and as we encourage others in their dating relationships—we were compelled to view dating as neither good nor evil. Instead, we perceived that dating is simply a social custom that requires believers to lean on the wisdom and guidance of the Holy Spirit. We believe that Christians can use the Word of God as a plumb line (see Amos 7:7-8), which measures, directs, and aligns their every action—moreover, their every relationship—with God's will.

IT'S SIMPLER THAN YOU THINK

One of the greatest challenges we've encountered in talking with and teaching singles about dating is semantic in nature. Because many people operate with different definitions of words such as *dating* and *courting*, confusion can easily arise as Christians attempt to build relationships.

When we first began to write on this topic, we felt it necessary to help single Christians define what a date really was. Our goal was to mitigate the uncertainties that seemed so prevalent in Christian circles.

We started by asking questions. In the process of researching how people defined dating, we discovered that out of one thousand single Christians ranging in age from fifteen to thirty, 90 percent had difficulty defining what it meant to date. Consider this telling comment from a twenty-two-year-old female, responding to the question, "How would you define a date?": "I don't know; it always seems sketchy when it's not clearly defined."

In my (Jeramy's) first book, *I Gave Dating a Chance*, I share some of the diverse definitions of dating people use. While one person may think dating is simply "spending time with special attention to a person of the opposite sex," another may consider it "time where you and your potential wife/husband go off with a group of friends to get to know each other in a better way."[1] It doesn't take a rocket scientist to recognize there could be trouble if these two tried to date. One is scoping out a potential spouse; the other is interested in a casual get-to-know-you.

Coming across so many divergent responses only encouraged us to help define the word *date* clearly and concisely. The definition that seemed to encompass all the possibilities singles shared with us was simpler than we thought. According to good old Webster, a date is merely a prearranged social engagement; a time set aside beforehand, social in nature.[2]

This definition includes the casual "let's grab coffee" yet leaves the candlelit dinner option open as well. It embraces group and one-on-one activities. It means dating happens more than people think. And it also means people have a greater responsibility to clearly define their intentions and their expectations to each other.

We believe that operating on a broader, simpler definition of dating takes some of the weight off activities that were meant to be lighthearted and fun. Take, for instance, dates such as school dances or formal work parties. These occasions should be a chance for men and women to interact over a fine dinner (or a cheesy version of one), good conversation, and maybe some music.

Single Christians should not have to turn down opportunities to enjoy the company of the opposite sex simply because their definition of a date is too stringent to allow for what might be a healthy way to get to know someone. Yet neither should singles view a broad definition of dating as an excuse to engage in worldly ways of interacting with the opposite sex.

The challenge with any freedom is to use it appropriately. Galatians 5:13 speaks to this pointedly: "You, my brothers, were called to be free. But do not use your freedom to indulge the sinful nature."[3] Basically, if you want the freedom to date, you have to accept the responsibilities that come with it, namely personal commitment to holiness and clear communication with others.

So now that we've cleared up some of the semantics, let's look at a few practical steps Christian singles can take to date well.

WHERE IT ALL STARTS

"'Love the Lord your God with all your heart and with all your soul and with all your mind.' This is the first and greatest commandment" (Matthew 22:37-38). Any discussion of the principles of healthy relationships must start here. There is nothing more important than establishing your first and greatest priority in life: to love the Lord your God. And not to love Him partially but to love Him with all that you are: body, spirit, and mind.

People often look to relationships to quiet an aching, restless heart that both needs to be loved and wants to love. But a relationship with any person, no matter how wonderful, will never satisfy this hunger inside you.

You may have noticed we mentioned that the heart both needs to be loved and wants to love. Let's start with the first part of that, the part in each person that yearns to be loved.

God forever answered the question of whether you are loved when He gave His Son on Calvary: "This is how God showed his love among us: He sent his one and only Son into the world that we might live through him" (1 John 4:9). John goes on to say, "In this way, love is made complete among us" (4:17). The broken, needy part of you seeking to give and receive love will only be sated by the love made complete among us through Christ.

David Wilcox, a profound poet and musician, sings about a break in the cup that holds love inside us. This break is caused by sin and makes us less able to give and receive love. When we seek fulfillment through human affection, we find that the break in our cup leaves us with a loveless void. Though drained and poured out, we still try to fill ourselves with the love of other, just as empty people.

Wilcox challenges us not to trade our emptiness for the emptiness of another but to go to the waterfall to be filled. We must plunge ourselves beneath the flood of God's love, which never runs dry. Christ Himself promised to give us living water. He said, "Whoever drinks the water I give him will never thirst. Indeed, the water I give him will become in him a spring of water welling up to eternal life"—a life filled with true Love (John 4:14). He is the source of love, and we must be right with Him before we can relate to others.

And most of us want to relate to others. God created within us a desire for companionship and fellowship. This is the second ache in our hearts, the yearning to give love.

Stuart Briscoe agrees. He said, "Scripture makes it very clear that our lives are lived in terms of relationships: with God and with human beings."[4] That is why immediately after Christ described the first and greatest commandment, He added, "The second is like it: 'Love your neighbor as yourself'" (Matthew 22:39).

This is the *second* commandment because without first embracing the perfect love God gives, we are incapable of loving others as ourselves. The trouble comes for most of us when we confuse the first and second commandments. We try to love others first, hoping they'll love us back and stop up the break in our cup, when what we need to do is love God, who then grants us the ability to love others.

Without a right relationship with Jesus, your relationships with others will not be whole. But with the complete, perfect love He died to give, you have everything to offer. Shirley Rice penned these powerful words: "Once you've been loved by God, you are loved completely, and you do not need to grasp anymore."[5] C. S. Lewis once claimed that if you put first things first, you get second and third things thrown in, but if you put second and third things first, you lose everything.[6]

If you want to have healthy relationships with others, put first things first. Love the Lord your God with all your heart, soul, and mind. And love your neighbor as yourself. This is where it all starts.

WHAT'S INSIDE

The second step in learning to date well involves discovering how to lean on and listen to the Holy Spirit. Left to our own devices in dating, many of us would succumb to temptation. In the search for love, some might even wander away from God. But fortunately, God promised He would never abandon us. He has not left us on our own, unable to determine which way to go.

In John 14:16-18, Jesus promised,

> "I will talk to the Father, and he'll provide you another
> Friend so that you will always have someone with you.
> This Friend is the Spirit of Truth. The godless world
> can't take him in because it doesn't have eyes to see
> him, doesn't know what to look for. But you know him
> already because he has been staying with you, and will
> even be *in* you!
>
> I will not leave you orphaned." (MSG)

Those dating in the "godless world" neither see nor respond to the Spirit. But Christians are indwelt by God Himself, the Holy Spirit, and can rely on Him to guide, instruct, and empower them. What an incredible truth!

In *Christian Theology*, Millard J. Erickson writes,

> Part of the efficacy of the Spirit's work is a result of [his] internality. Jesus had been a teacher and leader, but his influence was that of external word and example. The Spirit, however, is able to affect one more intensely because, dwelling within, he can get to the very center of one's thinking and emotions. By indwelling believers, the Spirit can lead them into all truth, as Jesus promised.[7]

Living inside us, the Spirit can get to the core of who we are and what we are doing, and yet we often underestimate that we have such an amazing source of power, truth, and direction. Some believe Christians should not date because they will be too tempted to sin, but this seems to undercut the Spirit's ability to lead a believer in an appropriate relationship with the opposite sex.

Galatians 5:16 proclaims, "Live by the Spirit, and you will not gratify the desires of the sinful nature." In *The Message*, Eugene Peterson translates the same verse like this: "Live freely, animated and motivated by God's Spirit. Then you won't feed the compulsions of selfishness."

As we strive to walk in step with the Spirit, our choices will reflect God's will and not our own. It follows that if we *date* in step with the Spirit, our relationship decisions will likewise honor God.

This does not mean that you will date perfectly. In fact, you may find that as you learn to walk with the Spirit, you'll become more aware of how you fail to listen to Him and obey His still, small voice of love. If this happens, be encouraged; you are in good company. No one relates to the opposite sex perfectly. All of us who have dated have made mistakes, and through learning from our failings, we have grown in our ability to follow God's commands and receive His grace.

Even if you continuously make bad decisions for some time, you always have the opportunity to ask the Holy Spirit to lead you from this point forward. You do not have to spend time in self-recrimination; right where you are, no matter how sinful or ugly, return to the Lord who waits with open arms to forgive and redeem.

But let us return to the idea of what it means to "live by the Spirit." Among other things, it involves knowing and recognizing His work. Though the roles of the Spirit are manifold, His work as teacher, counselor, and enabler are particularly important when it comes to relationship between the sexes.

The ministry of the Holy Spirit as teacher includes illuminating Scripture. Without the Spirit, we could neither know nor understand the Word. In 1 Corinthians 2, Paul describes the Spirit as searching the deep things of God, knowing the mind of God, and helping us understand what God has freely given. As you search the Scriptures with regard to dating and relationships, ask the Holy Spirit to illuminate the Word of God as well as prepare you to receive and understand it.

Jesus also promised that the Holy Spirit would be a counselor. With the coming of the Spirit, God fulfilled an ancient promise of Isaiah: "Whether you turn to the right or to the left, your ears will hear a voice behind you, saying, 'This is the way; walk in it'" (Isaiah 30:21). So when you are wondering which way to go, which step to take, or whether to date at all, lean on the Counselor who vows to disclose God's will.

Finally, the Spirit empowers and enables believers to desire and carry out the will of God. The apostle John uses the Greek word *perakletos* to describe this ministry of the Spirit. Dr. Richard Mayhue writes, "Christ was the enabling presence among the disciples' faltering weaknesses, and so would be the coming Holy Spirit promised to them by Christ as *perakletos*."[8] The most commonly used translation of *perakletos* is the Old English word *comforter*. From the Latin *con* (with) and *fortis* (strength), *perakletos* literally means "with strength." When we are weak, the Spirit comforts with strength.

In order to date well, we need to rely on the Spirit as teacher, counselor, and enabler. His strength is what we require to date with integrity and conviction. His advice is the best we can receive. His instruction allows us to search the deep things of God and apply them to our relationships with the opposite sex.

Dating well begins with defining your relationship with God and continues with learning to lean on and listen to the Holy Spirit.

WORTH BEING FOUND

The night before Valentine's Day, I (Jerusha) did a radio interview with a large Los Angeles station. After the host and I spoke for some time, he opened the lines for questions from the audience. All of the queries I fielded that night centered on how to find the "right" person. "Where are the godly men and women?" singles asked me. Their questions took me back to a time when I asked the same thing. The answer God gave surprised me, and I had to face some hard truths about myself in the process.

In college, a mentor of mine, Ruth, listened patiently as I confessed my concern about attracting all the wrong guys. "Where are all the godly men?" I lamented. Ruth took a risk and boldly challenged me: "Jerusha, before you can find someone worth finding, *you* must first become someone worth being found." Basically, I needed to work on myself before I could find someone with whom I could share a godly relationship. I needed to develop godly character qualities in myself before I could find them in someone else.

This is not to say that *all* single Christians who wonder how to find a godly companion need to step back and focus on their character as I did. But the reality is, it's a lot easier to focus outward and critique someone else than to evaluate your own life and make the changes needed to attract the right kind of person.

At our wedding, we received a card that included the message, "Marriage is not so much finding the right person as it is being the right person." We'd expand that to include all relationships, whether friendship, dating, or marriage.

We spent a great deal of time thinking about this topic before we wrote our second book, *He's HOT, She's HOT*. In that book, we boil down into three broad descriptors hundreds of godly character qualities one could develop or look for in a person of the opposite sex. Together, these traits define someone who's "H.O.T." In the pages of *HOT*, we deal extensively with these traits, but for now, let us give you a glimpse.

Do keep in mind as you read the following pages that on this side of heaven, you will never reach a point at which your character is fully developed. There will always be areas in which the Lord will mold and shape you anew. You can, however, begin to grow in the process of character development by thinking about the general traits we describe for you in this section.

The *H* in H.O.T. stands for holy. The Christian life is all about becoming holy, and Christian dating is about the same thing—becoming and looking for a person who is not only pursuing God but is passionate about being set apart for Him. That is what it means to be holy—to be spiritually pure and dedicated to the service of God. The word *holy* has taken on some pretty negative connotations in today's society. A friend of ours joked that nonbelievers think Christians become holy by being baptized in lemon juice—the holier the person gets, the more sour his expression becomes. But Christians' views of holiness can be just as skewed. We think of eating locusts, wearing robes, taking vows of poverty (or worse, celibacy!), and rising before dawn to fast and pray.

Yet the Word describes finding God in the *splendor* of His holiness (see 1 Chronicles 16:29; Psalm 29:2). It also encourages us, "As obedient children, let yourselves be pulled into a way of life shaped by God's life, a life energetic and blazing with holiness" (1 Peter 1:15, MSG).

The words *energetic* and *blazing* fly in the face of the common, yet misguided, perspectives on holiness. We don't want to imply that holiness is reserved for a select few who can "tough out" the real disciplines of the Spirit, either. Some believe only monks or ministers can attain holiness. Not so!

The Lord commands us five times—four in the Old Testament and once in the New—to be holy because He is holy (see Leviticus 11:44-45; 19:2; 20:7; 1 Peter 1:16). We are compelled to live a holy life because God Himself is holy. He does not merely set the standard; He is the standard.

Holiness is for all believers and has been made available to us by the blood of the Lamb and the indwelling of the Spirit. Holiness is one of God's principal designs for our life: "God did not call us to be impure, but to live a holy life" (1 Thessalonians 4:7). And holiness is active and awesome, changing us from the inside out and making us more like Christ.

As we become more like Him, we will not only be able to recognize others who are seeking Him with all they are, but we'll find ourselves drawn to those people. Someone who is serious about holiness won't join forces with someone who's any less committed. That's the nature of being holy.

Becoming a person worth being found starts with an understanding of and zeal for holiness. Holy people seek others who will spur them on to love and good deeds, as Scripture urges. And as holy men and women interact, they build one another up in Christ, sharpening each other and holding one another accountable.

The second trait we identified as essential to both cultivate and look for puts the spunk in H.O.T. The O stands for outrageous. An outrageous person uniquely and remarkably reflects God's image to the world. In fact, *outrageous* can be used synonymously with words such as *exceptional, extraordinary, special, memorable, marvelous, striking,* and *wonderful*.

Basically, becoming an outrageous person means capturing the truth that everyone—that *you*—have been fearfully and wonderfully designed by the Creator in His image (see Genesis 1:27; Psalm 139:14). It means living out God's intention that your body and spirit marvelously reveal His nature in a way only you can.

Becoming an outrageous person encompasses everything from developing your individual personality to taking care of your physical body. But fundamentally, being outrageous means living up to your God-given, uniquely wonderful potential.

A few words need to be inserted here about how our physicality impacts our relationships with the opposite sex. Earnest Christians often ask us whether physical attraction should play any role in their decision to get to know another person. In *HOT*, we look at how God describes people's physical appearance and how attractiveness influences others. (In the first book of the Bible alone, there are four references to individuals being drawn to one another's physical appearance. See Genesis 12:11-15; 24:16,67; 29:16-18; 39:6-7.)

We find that contemporary Christians, too, notice beauty or rugged good looks. Guess what? This is not sinful. In fact, it's part of God's plan to draw husbands and wives together. He wants spouses to delight in the gift of each other's bodies. If you haven't read Song of Solomon in a while, even a quick perusal will remind you of God's unashamed blessing of physical love in marriage.

The challenge in dating is to hold physical attraction in balance with the other characteristics—holiness and trustworthiness, among others—that one should pursue. Physical attraction is not everything, but it can be a component of being drawn to another person.

One needs to remember, however, that all forms of attraction ebb and flow, even for married lovers. James Dobson so skillfully describes this phenomenon in his book *What Wives Wish Their Husbands Knew About Women*: "Even when a man and woman love each other deeply and genuinely, they will find themselves supercharged on one occasion and . . . bland on another! However, their love is not defined by the highs and lows, but is dependent on a commitment of their will."[9] Lasting love prizes commitment first and attraction second.

God makes each of us differently so that we may not only enjoy His infinite creativity but also learn to love all that He loves. Each one of us reflects God's image in a special way; because of that, we are all—you are—remarkable in some way. Finding an outrageous person means appreciating that which God has marvelously revealed in each individual and discovering which personalities you are drawn to.

We once did a radio interview during which a man (we'll call him

Louie) who'd been married for over fifty years called the station. The host had invited people with "great love stories" to share their secrets of success. When asked, "How have you stayed happily married for so long?" Louie responded that he'd found a godly woman with whom he loved to spend time. After over five decades, they still delighted in one another's uniqueness and wanted to be together.

You cannot build a happy marriage with "just anyone." And though you need to look first for holiness reflected in someone's life, you must also determine whether or not you enjoy, delight in, and desire a person's companionship. You need to find someone you think is outrageous.

Both of us struggled at different times, believing we'd have to choose between marrying someone to whom we were attracted or someone sold out for God. Yet as we trusted the Lord, we found that He longed to give us both. We share a passion for holiness, and we love exploring the outrageous aspects of one another.

We've also built our relationship on the foundation of trust. Trustworthiness, the *T* in H.O.T., is the final characteristic that Christians should both develop and pursue in relationship with the opposite sex.

Darren, who once heard us dissect the H.O.T. traits, related this heartbreaking story, urging us to exhort singles to become and find trustworthy mates. Darren married a woman he thought to be both godly and attractive. He never suspected that she led another life, running up thousands of dollars on credit cards for which he never knew she'd applied. She brought their family to the brink of financial and relational ruin. Though Darren pursued counseling and believed that his wife could learn to be trustworthy, she ultimately left him, unwilling or unable to admit her wrong. Sadly, Darren's story is not unique. We've ached with many who've shared their stories of betrayal. Godly relationships must be built on a foundation of trust.

In order to get a handle on what it means to be trustworthy, we broke the word down into three different categories. A trustworthy person is at once *authentic, honest,* and *reliable.*

Put most simply, authenticity means being who you claim to be — being "real." An authentic life displays consistency and commitment. It reveals a pattern of behavior that reflects a person's deepest beliefs. For Christians, authenticity and a lifestyle of sin are incongruous. All believers will sin; Christians may even persist in sin for some time. Yet authentic followers of Christ ultimately respond to the conviction of the Holy Spirit and grow by repenting from their sin.

In *The Calvary Road*, Roy Hession writes, "The first effect of sin in us is always to make us hide; with the result that we are pretending, we are wearing a mask, we are not real with either God or man. And, of course, neither God nor man can fellowship with an unreal person."[10]

You simply cannot have true fellowship or build a healthy relationship if either you or someone you're dating is inauthentic. Look for and be a person who lives out his or her convictions.

| **What Do You Think?** | Do you agree that inauthentic relationships cannot be healthy? Why or why not? |

The Lord speaks boldly about the second component of trustworthiness: honesty. Proverbs 12:22 reveals,

> The LORD detests lying lips,
> but he delights in men who are truthful.

As He hates dishonesty and rejoices in truth, so should we. This might seem like a no-brainer to some of you out there, but you'd be shocked by how many singles we've helped to get out of relationships that amounted to nothing more than a web of lies. Keeping with God's standards, Christians should neither deceive nor engage in relationships with those who habitually do so.

Finally, living a trustworthy life involves staying true to your promises. In other words, it means being *reliable*. Can people count on you? Do you do what you say you will?

Jesus tells the parable of two sons who work for their father. The first son tells his father he will go out to work but never does. The second son makes no promise but later decides to go to work. The Lord reserves harsher judgment for the first son, who does not keep his word (see Matthew 21:28-31). God wants us to follow through with what we promise.

In Luke 16:10, Jesus says, "Whoever can be trusted with very little can also be trusted with much." Before you give someone your heart (which is worth much), see if that person can be trusted with very little. Show others that you are reliable as well. Then you will be ready to both give and care for much.

So as we've shown, the third step to healthy dating encompasses becoming and finding someone who is "H.O.T." Though holiness, outrageousness, and trustworthiness are three traits we consider foundational, there are other righteous attributes you will want to seek out in others and develop in yourself. We encourage you to pursue the qualities we've described, as well as other godly traits, so that you will be "someone worth being found." Perhaps then you will be ready to find someone and take the fourth step in dating well: discovering the freedom that boundaries within dating bring.

"Eternal vigilance is the price of freedom."[11] One of the most important aspects of dating well involves setting and maintaining appropriate boundaries. Most Christians recognize the need to define clear standards for physical purity but we'd like to highlight the necessity of working out strong emotional boundaries as well.

Boundaries protect you from the scars that come from premature intimacy. Inappropriate intimacy—whether physical, spiritual, or emotional—can prevent you from enjoying healthy intimacy later in life. Solid standards also protect you from the world's lies about what relationships should look like.

But more important, boundaries are essential because God commands that we preserve purity. His charges to us to "keep vigilant watch over your heart" (Proverbs 4:23, MSG) and that "it is God's will that you be sanctified: that you should avoid sexual immorality" (1 Thessalonians 4:3) make clear that the purity of both our hearts and bodies must be defended—and vigilantly, at that.

In my first book, *I Gave Dating a Chance*, I (Jeramy) wrote, "Purity is not just about touching. It's about your mind and your heart. It concerns your whole lifestyle. . . . The more purely you think, the more purely you will act."[12]

If we are to safeguard our purity, we must carefully ponder standards that will prevent us from compromise. To set healthy emotional and physical boundaries, we recommend you start with knowing yourself. We don't mean this in a new-age way but in a very practical one.

Perhaps you know that talking about marriage, sharing past sins, or discussing deep spiritual matters draws you close to someone rather quickly; you may want to consider curtailing or avoiding conversation about such topics. Likewise, identifying the things that arouse you physically and taking a step back from there to draw your lines will also set you on the way to establishing some healthy boundaries.

Don't cop out and claim, "I can't tell what causes me to become intimate with someone." We can feel it in our bodies when we draw near to someone physically. We sense it in our hearts when we're "falling" into emotional involvement with another person. Be wise enough to observe yourself and consider asking others to help you distinguish how you relate.

After acknowledging those things that lead you into closeness with someone, decide what lines you will draw *before* you get into any potentially compromising situations. Isaiah wrote,

> Because the Sovereign LORD helps me,
> I will not be disgraced.
> Therefore have I set my face like flint,
> and I know I will not be put to shame. (Isaiah 50:7)

Isaiah experienced no shame because he determined ahead of time to accept the Lord's help and remain as unyielding as flint.

Relationships can be virtually shame-free when people set definite boundaries and follow through with action. We advise that once you've set up your boundaries, you write them down. This small step helps cement your thoughts with commitment. Additionally, a tangible reminder can sustain you when tempted.

Asking someone to partner with you in maintaining your boundaries will further strengthen your steadfastness. We recommend you seek an older, more mature believer to hold you accountable. An outside observer can often tell more quickly than you can that a relationship is headed for trouble. If you are honest and willing to listen to an accountability partner, you'll have a huge advantage in preserving your purity.

If you enter a relationship, communicate your boundaries clearly. Don't beat around the bush when talking about physical or emotional standards. Should you feel too embarrassed to discuss kissing or saying "I love you," you may want to reconsider whether you're ready for a relationship.

Finally, admit when you've stepped over the line. Ask God to convict you. Regularly revisit your list and pray over it. Actively turn, resetting your course. We recognize this is not easy to do. We all make mistakes while dating, yet some come with more far-reaching consequences than others. We do not want this exhortation to repent to come off in a trite, "fix-all" way. Rather, we mean to encourage you that by His grace, no matter how many times you flub up, you *can* turn and begin anew.

To wrap up this section, we'd like to help those of you who may not know what setting emotional boundaries looks like. We often have questions about this important issue, and we hope that the following suggestions will aid you in creating some limits that will vigilantly guard your heart.

One example of emotional boundaries includes choosing wisely what to talk about (such as marriage, deep spiritual matters, and so forth). Some subjects foster deeper closeness more so than others.

Opting to talk less may be another standard you set. Proverbs 10:19 reveals, "When words are many, sin is not absent." The more you speak, the greater your chances are for premature emotional intimacy.

Focusing on listening and asking questions that direct a conversation will also protect you and your date from divulging too much too soon. Beware of the reality that many Christians trade physical intimacy for emotional and spiritual closeness. Those raised in the church may try to avoid sexual immorality at all costs while failing to guard their hearts. We've watched Christians who've never touched experience deep pain in separating because they've forged powerful emotional bonds. Intimate acts of worship such as praying together can draw you closer than many physical expressions of affection.

Emotional purity can be preserved, but it requires some effort. We recommend that people get creative in their activities and conversations. Instead of the two of you renting a movie and sitting on the couch, invite friends to watch and then discuss the movie with you (and, let's face it, at the end of the night, it's best if your beau leaves at the same time as the rest of the group). Read books together or listen to CDs and talk about them. If it's tough at the beginning to do some of these things, take heart. The fruits of intentional activities and conversation will be sweet.

By the way, whether or not you choose to date, these tips for emotional purity will strengthen your friendships as well as prepare you for marriage, should that be God's will for your life.

If you'd like more information on emotional or physical boundaries, we discuss these issues at greater length in our first three books. For now, let's take a look at the fifth step to dating well: conscientious communication.

CLARITY, NOT CONFUSION

Imagine two people ready to date but with divergent hopes for an evening together. Perhaps, as we mentioned before, they'll be attending a work party or school dance. The gentleman spends hours planning an elaborate night full of surprises. She, on the other hand, wants to spend more time with her friends or coworkers than she does with him.

Or consider flipping that equation. Imagine a woman investing lots of time and money in a fancy dress, makeup, and other accessories. But when her date arrives, he's dressed casually and appears nonchalant.

Christians should be free to enjoy time with the opposite sex. But does this mean they are exempted from the responsibility of communicating clearly, respecting the feelings and expectations of their companions, or generally loving their neighbors as themselves? As Paul might say, "By no means!"

In addition to working on your relationship with the Lord, developing and pursuing characteristics of godliness, and establishing boundaries for your dating relationships, you will want to learn to communicate well. Misunderstandings can be an incredibly destructive force in any relationship, and most relational mix-ups occur when people fail to communicate openly their intentions and desires.

Therefore, we recommend that people invest time in learning how to communicate well. Acquiring some basic communication skills can go a long way in clearing up the confusion and sometimes heartbreak that can accompany dating relationships.

For instance, studies show that only 7 percent of a given message is content, while tone accounts for 38 percent and nonverbal cues 55 percent.[13] According to this research, *how* you say something really matters. While this probably doesn't surprise any of us (we've all felt the sting of sarcasm or doubted someone's words because of the way they spoke and acted), most of us do not *act* on the knowledge that nonverbal cues and tone greatly determine how others receive our words.

Ask close friends about your communication and listen to any suggestions they might have to help you improve. Be willing to hear some hard things, if need be, and work on making changes that bring your tone and nonverbal cues into agreement with the content of your message.

This principle clearly applies to dating relationships. Picture a breakup during which the person breaking up rests a hand on the knee of or sits with an arm around the other, claiming they should be apart. No matter what might be said, the message could easily be misconstrued.

This is just one foundational truth about communication that can profoundly impact your ability to date well. In our book *Define the Relationship* we outline others and describe a tool we've found extraordinarily effective in maintaining godly relationships. You've probably heard of it; it's called the "DTR." Most simply, DTR is a conversation that defines a relationship. It is:

> a communication tool used to assess a relationship's strengths and weaknesses. . . . [It] helps two people determine their shared level of interest as well as their intentions for the relationship's future. A DTR can be used either to set the course for a couple or end the journey. It can and should be utilized to maintain a healthy relationship during its natural growth process.[14]

Because it required an entire book to explain key aspects for a successful DTR, such as when to DTR and how to employ the tool in various situations (setting boundaries, going to the next level in a relationship, or breaking up), we cannot fully explore the topic here.

A word of warning: DTRs can be overdone. We discuss this at length in the book, but we felt it necessary to include here. People can get obsessed with words and labels or with knowing exactly what's going on. We strongly recommend that you approach DTRs with a balanced perspective on what they can accomplish.

That said, let us emphasize that the primary goal of a DTR is to bring a couple to a shared vision for where the relationship stands and where it is headed. DTRs seek to promote clarity and eliminate as much confusion as possible, which is invaluable for good communication in dating.

PREDECISIONS

You cannot date well without a plan. Furthermore, without focus and intentionality, you'll find yourself on meaningless dates and in unfulfilling relationships. This may sound harsh, but it's true nonetheless.

What Do You Think?	Jeramy and Jerusha say, "You cannot date well without a plan." What does that mean to you, and do you agree? What experiences have you had that either negate or confirm this statement?

We cannot stress enough the importance of making some basic decisions before you head out on a date — or into a dating relationship. In the section on boundaries, we highlighted the necessity of drawing your lines before you find yourself in a potentially compromising situation. We want to take that a step further and recommend that you carefully plan your dates. We encourage you to make predecisions, or choices made ahead of time, that "prevent you from walking blindly into dangerous situations [and] also help you to wisely evaluate each dating opportunity."[15]

In order to steer clear of potentially compromising situations, deciding ahead of time where you will go and with whom you will be is nonnegotiable. You act differently depending on where you are and with whom you are surrounded. You will make far better split-second choices if you've predecided to be in good company and in a place that encourages you to be a man or woman of God.

Planning also takes into account your intentions for the future of a relationship. If you want a casual date to simply have fun in the company of an enjoyable brother or sister in the Lord, you could catch a good flick with friends or attend an event together. On the other hand, if you really want to get to know someone better or take your relationship to the next level, something such as a movie or a loud sporting event might not be the best bet.

Another aspect of predeciding is resolving to follow through. Just planning to do something does not assure dating success. You must carry out the plan to succeed. It's one thing to have convictions; it's another to live them out.

While outlining this book, we spoke with a friend who had recently begun dating a girl from work. We probed a bit, curious about her relationship with the Lord. He told us that she professed faith but that he wanted to get to the nitty-gritty of how she lived, not just what she claimed she believed. His wisdom can be an exhortation to you, as it was to us. Live out your own convictions and find someone who does the same.

We've discovered that you can follow through a lot easier if you've run your arrangements by someone else before you head out on a date. Scripture teaches plainly that "plans fail for lack of counsel" (Proverbs 15:22). Let someone you trust know what you've set up. If they caution you, consider returning to the drawing board. If they give an unreserved green light, go and have fun! Moreover, articulating what you've planned will help keep you on track and can provide much-needed accountability after your date.

The Word proclaims, "Those who plan what is good find love and faithfulness" (Proverbs 14:22). That verse is no guarantee that if you devise a good plan, you'll find the love of your life but rather that you'll find God's love and faithfulness sustaining you and blessing you as you date.

THE LAST WORD

As a final step in dating well, we encourage you to reevaluate often and thoroughly. You may find that after dating for some time, your convictions have slipped and you've allowed more, planned less, focused more on yourself than the other person, or neglected to build your godly character and relationship with the Lord. If any of these components of healthy dating suffer, all will begin to decline.

Thousands of years ago, Socrates asserted that the "unexamined life is not worth living." Jesus affirmed this truth in His ministry, and the writers of the Epistles further emphasized the need for reflection on one's actions. Take time to step back and contemplate your relationships (by the way, this can strengthen your friendships as well!). Ask the Lord to reveal any way in which you've stepped over the lines or dishonored Him in your interaction with the opposite sex.

Maybe you don't even need to pray about what you've done. You may know that you've entertained or engaged in sin. Repent of what He reveals or that for which you've already felt conviction. Jesus told the adulterous woman in John 8:11 to "go now and leave your life of sin." His forgiveness is freely given and complete, yet He asks us to leave our sinful ways and follow Him.

Don't allow things to start or continue to slide. Relationships require effort, and without some work on your part, erosion will occur. Erosion occurs when forces "destroy by slow disintegration."[16] In the natural world, water or wind can eat away at land and foliage. In relationships, forces such as conflict and the abandonment or relaxing of boundaries can wear down a couple's once healthy interaction. Protect your relationships from erosion by consistent assessment. You need to do more than start well to date successfully.

Most likely, there will come a time in all of your relationships that will require you to reorganize your priorities and reestablish your boundaries. We will not relate to each other perfectly this side of heaven, yet we always have the opportunity to evaluate and renew our commitments to the Lord.

REALITY CHECK

In order to help flesh out the principles and guidelines we've been discussing, we'd like to offer you the advice we'd give if confronted with three distinct relationship dilemmas.

An important note: These scenarios, common to each of the chapters in this book, do not take into account every detail about the lives of those involved. If we had more information, some of our recommendations might alter, but as the scenarios were given to us, we've evaluated them.

Jenny and David

In the first set of circumstances, we meet Jenny and David, high school juniors. We don't know their ages, but assuming they did not skip grades or get held back, Jenny and David would be somewhere between fifteen and seventeen. (Don't scoff at the younger end of that spectrum: Jerusha was fifteen her junior year and *mortified* that she couldn't get a driver's license until November of that year!) We're informed that friends have told Jenny and David they'd be a cute couple.

The first thing we'd recommend is that these two ignore their friends' pressurized comments. Jenny and David should not be motivated to date simply because others think their personalities or physical appearances complement one another. In fact, these two may have a harder time getting to know each other honestly if they focus on what others project about their potential.

If Jenny and David want to pursue getting to know one another better, the second thing we advise is that they clarify what their parents' rules for dating are. Both have "involved, caring Christian parents," so Jenny and David have a head start when approaching their parents about opposite-sex relationships.

Whatever expectations their parents have of Jenny and David, these two need to obey. Still under their "caring" authority, Jenny and David must heed their directives. This may be unpopular with some, but if Jenny or David's parents do not allow them to date because of their age or maturity, there's just no other godly option than to respect their parents' wishes.

Let's assume, however, that both sets of parents allow their children to date. Jenny and David would still benefit from a conversation with their folks about curfews, boundaries both outside and in the home, and so on. This kind of conversation will provide clarity for Jenny and David and can facilitate nonconfrontational interaction among family members and a boyfriend or girlfriend who might be invited to the home. Additionally, it can give the parents confidence in their son or daughter's commitments and open lines of communication for the future.

As their parents take an active, though not overly active, role in their relationship (overinvolvement can have major downfalls), we'd counsel Jenny and David—as we'd advise *any* couple—to apply what we've recommended previously about defining their relationship with the Lord, developing their character, leaning on the Spirit, establishing boundaries, learning to communicate, and planning and reevaluating their relationship.

Finally, taking into account their stage of life and their youth, we'd ask Jenny and David to get to know each other well on a friendship level before they begin talking about or pursuing romance. Having watched for thirteen years, we've determined that we're not huge fans of exclusive high school relationships. Maintaining a healthy one-on-one relationship for any length of time requires discernment and patience, among other qualities. These virtues often come with age.

We like to see younger singles enjoy events such as homecoming or prom but not become completely wrapped up in a relationship. If Jenny and David decide to go on some one-on-one dates, we'd encourage them to keep them completely "above reproach" (see 1 Timothy 3:2), meaning they avoid compromising their commitments to the Lord or to their parents. They can best do this by choosing casual settings for their dates (probably no candlelit dinners on the beach for these two), being in public places or near other people in their family's homes, and keeping their conversation away from emotionally bonding subjects.

Group dating would also be a great bet for Jenny and David. Some think that group dating is limited to courtship models, but we believe a healthy model of dating in general includes time spent in groups.

With caring, involved parents on their side and faithfulness to godly standards, we believe Jenny and David can get to know and enjoy each other on dates.

On a more general front, we'd like to answer the question that is begged by presenting such a scenario. Can young people date well? Yes, but with caution. Younger daters should be aware of temptations to become obsessed or get too close too soon. Not all sixteen-year-olds are mature enough to date, but when it comes down to it, neither are all thirty-year-olds! Regardless of the dater's age, dating well requires wisdom and responsibility.

Steve and Rachel

Steve and Rachel, students at a secular university, find themselves attracted to one another. Rachel, described as a new believer, and Steve, a Christian since high school, come from non-Christian families.

Right off the bat, we'd tell Steve and Rachel that no one should be rejected simply because he or she is a new Christian. Some new believers grow in their faith so rapidly and with such devoted passion that they explode into a vibrant relationship with the Lord that keeps pace with those who've been raised in Christian homes.

We'd probably relate to Steve and Rachel our story and explain how our age difference, as well as our divergent levels of maturity, impacted our relationship. When we met, Jerusha had recently recommitted her life to the Lord. Jeramy, on the other hand, was six years older and had been working in ministry for a while. During that time, his faith had grown considerably.

Some might have counseled Jeramy to either wait until Jerusha was older and had more time to mature or to reconsider dating her altogether. But after some initial conversation and interaction, we discovered that we definitely wanted to date and that we shared a vision for the future as well. Just because it seems one person is more mature than the other does not mean a godly relationship cannot develop.

It's possible that Steve and Rachel may have a healthier relationship because of Rachel's recent conversion. She may have a more earnest commitment to the Lord because of her newfound life passion. This we cannot know.

The question we'd then pose to Steve and Rachel would be whether they would encourage one another in faith or find they pulled one another down. The scenario did not indicate why Steve and Rachel became attracted to one another, but if they articulated primarily shallow reasons, we'd advise against pursuing a relationship at this time.

If, however, they admired one another on a deeper level—in any number of combinations of spiritual, emotional, and physical aspects—we'd again recommend proceeding with caution (you will notice this is a theme for our advice!)

Neither Steve's nor Rachel's parents can offer the kind of spiritual encouragement and advice they would need to conduct a godly relationship, as they themselves do not know the Lord. This does not mean, however, that Steve and Rachel should discount everything their parents might have to say about relationships. They should listen with discernment and weigh whatever their folks might recommend against what the Bible teaches.

Steve and Rachel can also find spiritual mothers and fathers in mentors and/or pastors. We'd counsel both of them to seek out an older person of faith from whom—and with whom—they might grow. We'd advise this whether or not they decide to get to know one another in a dating relationship.

Developing strong ties of accountability with older Christians, as well as gleaning from their experiences and wisdom, will help Steve and Rachel stand firm in their convictions while providing the missing element of Christian family. There's a funny yet poignant message on a greeting card that reads, "Friends are God's excuse for family." The family of God in the form of mentors, pastors, and peers can help Steve and Rachel develop and maintain a healthy relationship.

This couple, like all others, should apply the principles we recommend for dating well. In summary, Steve and Rachel should focus themselves in all the ways we've just described and firmly root them-selves before jumping into a relationship.

Denise

A thirty-year-old businesswoman, Denise stays active in her church family and invests time in friendships and activities. She's never dated much but senses that time is running out; she nurses a deep desire for marriage and children.

Denise might very well be any one of our close single friends. The first thing we affirm in such a situation is the genuine longing for a spouse and kids. There's nothing wrong with yearning for these things and praying that God would direct her path to that end.

The question really seems to be, Can Denise initiate in any way? Can she put her profile on the Internet and hope for the best? Can she attend singles' events and develop relationships that might eventually blossom into romance?

We see no problem with Denise pursuing these things, providing she balances this aspect of her life with other pursuits. If her desire for marriage and children consumes all of her thoughts and time, she may be idolizing these things. Prayerfully, Denise can determine whether her intentions and actions please the Lord.

Some Christians like Denise feel they should do nothing, waiting on God to bring Mr. or Miss Right to them. Others go off the deep end, asking every single person they meet to go out on a date. It's one thing to pursue a desire; it's another to become obsessed with it, manipulating circumstances to get what one wants.

We would encourage Denise to initiate in healthy ways. At different points, we have counseled single friends to look into Christian websites, in part because we've rejoiced while witnessing the godly marriages of two couples who met through online dating services for believers.

We also believe church is a great place to meet others. If the singles' group at Denise's church feels like a meat market, then by all means, she shouldn't feel obligated to attend. But there *are* some thriving, God-centered singles' ministries.

If Denise feels intimidated by her lack of experience, she can get to know some couples, see how they interact, and ask questions about their dating. She could also get hold of some resources, such as books, tapes, magazines, and websites—dating and relationships are discussed everywhere!

The last topic we'd broach with Denise is whether she's come to terms with the question, Is God enough? If God says no to her request for a family, will she be okay? Logically, she may know that God is the all-sufficient One. But if she's to trust Him completely, that knowledge must fall from her head to her heart.

God can and will satisfy not just Denise's desires, but the longings of every person reading this book. He does not merely have the answers; He *is* the answer. We pray that as you make decisions about dating and relationships, He will grant you wisdom and joy in the journey.

THE PURPOSEFUL PATH: AN OVERVIEW

Definition

The Purposeful Path claims that young adults who love the Lord and long to please Him can date in a healthy way. Not everyone *has* to date, but single Christians *can* enjoy appropriate dating relationships if they approach the practice with God's perspective and guidelines. These guidelines include pursuing holiness, trustworthiness, and support from friends and family.

Distinctives

- Single Christians should not have to turn down opportunities to enjoy the company of the opposite sex, such as the prom or a movie night; these may be great opportunities to get to know a brother or sister in Christ.

- If you want the freedom to date, you have to accept the responsibilities that come with it, namely personal commitment to holiness and clear communication with others.

- Pursuing emotional and physical purity is essential if you want a healthy dating relationship.

- Purposeful dating requires forethought, good judgment, and good communication to make solid decisions. If you desire to seriously date, think carefully about whom you've chosen and why.

Key Verses

- Psalm 19:7-8

- Galatians 5:13

- Matthew 22:37-38

- Isaiah 30:21

- 1 Thessalonians 4:7

- Proverbs 4:23

- Proverbs 15:22

Key Benefits

- This approach allows you to rely on the Spirit to make good decisions. You can find the love of your life without following any particular formula.

- In the process of finding the love of your life, you can pursue a holy life and holy relationships while dating (even casual dating).

- You will learn to communicate well with people because purposeful dating requires frequent and quality communication.

Potential Problems

- Establishing boundaries, both emotional and physical, can be hard, and balancing them can be just as difficult. Some Christians who have lived a physically pure life can experience deep pain in breaking up because they've traded physical intimacy for powerful emotional bonds. Be careful of engaging in intimate acts of worship, such as praying together, because they can draw you closer than many physical expressions of affection can.

- Because this is a broad definition of dating, be careful not to use it as an excuse to engage in worldly ways of interacting with the opposite sex.

- While focusing on becoming the "right" person, some people may become obsessed with it and end up with ridiculous expectations for themselves and others. Remember to operate in an environment of grace.

HOW THIS ALL COMES TOGETHER

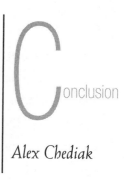

Conclusion

Alex Chediak

IN PREPARING THIS BOOK, MY DESIRE WAS TO PROVIDE A RESOURCE for Christians of any age, including parents, to gain an understanding of the main views held on the issue of romance among singles and the process they take toward marriage. I also hoped that Christians with different upbringings or inclinations could gain a greater understanding of each other and perhaps, in God's providence, be able to experience a God-centered relationship that leads to marriage. In my own relationship with my new bride, we had to communicate about our intentions and differing presuppositions as we interacted. With an increasing number of single adult Christians, I imagine that will be the case for many of you reading this book as well. I hope this book will increase your level of respect for those who see the issue differently than you do.

This is the end of the contributors' portion but not the end of the discussion. What I'd like to do now is try to summarize the areas of agreement and the areas of disagreement among the contributors in this book and then offer some suggestions for what to do with all of this.

AREAS OF AGREEMENT

The contributors were committed to the Scriptures as the authority in all matters, including the path to marriage. So with the Scriptures in mind, all contributors agreed that Christians should not marry or even date non-Christians. They also gladly distanced themselves from our culture's increasing affinity for casual hookups and breakups. They affirmed that Christians must live and "do relationships" in a manner that is clearly different from the world's approach. Perhaps the increasing decay in our culture with respect to casual sex—widely noted by both believers and unbelievers[1]—set the backdrop for the enormous success of Josh Harris's 1997 book. It seems that the *kind* of dating Harris rejected is something all five contributors would kiss good-bye.

The contributors also agreed that Christian families and social groups should play a role in the relationships of singles, though they differed on the importance of their participation. In the case of high schoolers Jenny and David, for example, all contributors agreed they should see themselves as being under the caring authority of their parents. This notion is more often questioned by older singles who, perhaps because of financial independence, place a greater emphasis on relational independence. They see themselves as less accountable to parents and their dating or sexual behavior as part of their "private life"—safely removed from the pesky imposition of others. All contributors, however, noted the dangers associated with singles, whether young or old, considering themselves completely independent from parents (although most of the contributors recognized that there aren't always "functioning" parents available, in which case alternatives were suggested).

Today, there are more single adult Christians in Western society than ever before. Lauren Winner alluded to the fact that the average

age of men and women getting married for the first time has increased in recent history. Indeed, the numbers are somewhat astonishing. In the U.S. since 1960, the average age of women has increased from twenty to twenty-five and of men from twenty-three to twenty-seven.[2] And despite the dangers of complete independence, many of these singles are living on their own. While in the 1950s nearly 80 percent of Americans lived in the home of a married couple, today that figure has dropped to 50 percent.[3] What all these numbers mean is that there is a higher percentage of adults in our culture who don't currently live in the context of a traditional, nuclear family and thus in many cases seek family by other means. The success of television programs such as *Friends* exhibits this pattern (the worldly lifestyles of the program's characters notwithstanding). No doubt the church has an opportunity and a responsibility to minister to singles in many new ways, including putting a greater emphasis on modeling what it means to be a husband, a wife, a father, and a mother. In addition, Christian parents and friends can provide important support to singles well into their young adult years. Christians inherently hunger for community, and community inherently provides a structure for transparency and accountability, which are so crucial for combating the innumerable challenges associated with relationships, including the temptation for sexual sin.

Some would say the rise in the marriage age and the extraordinarily high number of Christian singles are linked to the rising number of participants in graduate education programs and the like, but surely this can't be the only factor.[4] Something could be said for the widespread rejection of the family, in part from feminist quarters, in the 1970s and the present lack of institutions, particularly in American life, that foster male familial involvement.[5] Add to this the glorification of perpetual adolescence and independence in the world of television (consider

Seinfeld and *Friends*), the rise in couples living together before marriage, and, sadly, the increasing acceptance of this practice among professing Christians.[6] When these things are considered, a more complete picture becomes clear. We must cultivate a healthy respect, appreciation, and desire for Christian marriages—and we've got to share that respect with our youth. As most of the contributors stated (though they differed on the details), the possibility of marriage ought to set the tenor and framework of any premarital activity.

To carry the discussion further, singles need to recover a sense of the normalcy not just of marriage but also of the formation of families. Marriage and procreation are at the heart of a mature, flourishing society. The Genesis account shows God's intention that adult men and women live in pairs, not only for emotional fulfillment but also to form fruitful unions—spiritually, emotionally, and physically. The desire for emotional fulfillment points inward—the longing to enhance *my* life. The desire for a fruitful union inherently points outward—the longing to give of myself to create and nurture life, both in my spouse and in our children, and to in a sense pay back the gift of life by propagating the human race. Since 1960, the nation's birthrate has fallen by almost 50 percent to a historic low of 66.9 births per 1,000 women between the ages of 15 and 44 in 2003.[7] Sociologist Bradford Wilcox has noted that Christians are also contributing to this trend.[8] Deliberate, lifelong childlessness on the part of Christians often reveals marriages fueled by the drive for mere emotional fulfillment and outright moral rebellion against God's design.[9] In the Scriptures, children are welcomed as a gift from God (see 2 Samuel 6:23; Psalm 127:3-5). Many Christian singles need to recover a concept of adulthood that includes not just the completion of an educational curriculum or the landing of a stable job but also marriage and, in God's timing, fatherhood or motherhood.

But what about the gift of celibacy? After all, Paul says it is better to be single in 1 Corinthians 7. But Jesus qualifies this with language of "he who is able to accept it, let him accept it" (Matthew 19:12).[10] And for the majority of us, "It is better to marry than to burn with passion" (1 Corinthians 7:9). The gift of celibacy, then, needs to be seen as marked, at least in part, by a level of comfort with the thought of forgoing sexual companionship and the emotional pleasures of marriage.[11] So those with the glorious gift of celibacy ought not be dating merely for companionship. And their celibacy ought to be prized and honored in the church, to whom they are a gift. On the flipside, many single adults, particularly men, are in their state because of passivity, a fear of commitment, or a desire to maintain independence at all costs. And this should be graciously confronted with balanced wisdom considering the details of each case.

And what about the notion that churches cater exclusively to "cooing couples and nuclear families," as Lauren Winner put it? Where this happens, such narrow-mindedness ought to be critiqued and lovingly discouraged. We must maintain the truths in tension that while the call to marriage and family is the typical lot of adult believers, the institution of the biological family itself is not the ultimate reality. We will not be married in heaven (see Matthew 22:30), and Christ divides many families here on earth (see Luke 12:53). Moreover, in Christ, we are all family in the truest, most ultimate sense of the word (see Matthew 12:50). The nuclear family needs attention, but the church must incarnate the principle of Galatians 3:28 by never treating singles as second-class citizens in the kingdom. Only God knows the reason for their singleness; while we can help them assess motives and priorities, only God can judge their hearts. Regardless, community in the true family is the call to every Christian—those with the gift of celibacy for life, those who should seek marriage, and married people alike.

AREAS OF DISAGREEMENT

Both Jeramy and Jerusha Clark's and Lauren Winner's essays highlight the possibility of Christians in high school getting to know one another through group dates or activities such as homecoming or prom. Both essays emphasize the same principles regarding Jenny and David's scenario: the importance of abiding by parental restrictions and guidelines, the need to avoid undue emotional bonding, the need to guard against sexual temptation, and the value of employing group dates that render one-on-one interactions more rare than regular.

Meanwhile, the other contributors agree that any dating whatsoever on the part of Jenny and David would be ill-advised. The interaction among high schoolers is the source of greatest disagreement among the five approaches.

The differences in approaches to Rachel and Steve's scenario are interesting in several respects. First, there is a difference in the extent to which Rachel and Steve's parents' involvement is deemed reasonable or desirable. Lauren Winner emphasizes the role of older adults at a local church over and above parental involvement. The Clarks note that because the parents don't know the Lord, they would be unable to offer spiritual encouragement, but that Rachel and Steve should nevertheless weigh with discernment input from their parents. Rick Holland suggests they should consult with their parents, noting God's ability to use them regardless of their lack of faith, and in addition submit their desires to the wisdom of godly leadership at their church. Douglas Wilson and Jonathan Lindvall go even farther, suggesting that the relationship be conducted under the authority of Rachel's parents, particularly her father.

Second, the contributors have different views of how Rachel might become spiritually ready for marriage. Of the five contributors, Holland is the only one who suggests the wisest course might be for Rachel to be discipled in her faith before considering romance. This is consistent with his guided approach, which emphasizes Christian maturity as the chief prerequisite for marital readiness. The other contributors perhaps see the process of premarital activity as an inherently maturing institution (recall the example of the Clarks' own romance, the cruciform of Christian love that Lauren Winner describes, and the Christlike sanctifying influence that Wilson has elsewhere discussed[12]).

The responses to Denise's scenario highlight one more noteworthy difference among the contributors (which also arises elsewhere in their essays): the extent to which it is okay for women to initiate relationships. This is part of a long-standing debate among believers, the scope of which is far larger than this book. A sense that masculinity automatically denotes a man's obligation to initiate is a key component to Holland's, Wilson's, and Lindvall's view. The need for male initiation seems less urgent for the Clarks and Winner. However, Wilson, Holland, and the Clarks note several ways that a woman can, as Wilson puts it, "look for a husband without chasing one."

WHAT DO YOU DO WITH ALL OF THIS?

So how do you apply all of this? First, I hope you have an increased appreciation for other Christians who use different terminology than you do; they may not be very different from you after all. A great deal of understanding can be gained by hearing another's perspective and by looking for common ground rather than just common language. Second, different views on this topic are often reflections of a greater emphasis placed on certain principles. For example, all contributors agree that parental involvement is a good thing. So the difference is in degree, not principle, when the courtship and betrothal views are compared to the others. All but the betrothal essay, for example, address the possibility of the abuse of parental oversight.

Different views naturally appeal to Christians with different backgrounds, predispositions, or stages in life. Many teens who are several years away from marriageable age need to be reminded of the dangers of dating too soon and too intensely. Fortunately, warnings against impulsive and premature dating come from all contributors in this volume. Courtship is more amenable to Christians who have a strong community of faith and/or an extended family network, but it becomes more difficult to live out in detail if you're thirty-something and living away from home. Nevertheless, many of the principles of community involvement and support can be incorporated, though they perhaps will take more deliberate effort. Contemporary dating approaches lend themselves to the dangers of immature, directionless dating, which can lead to emotional pain or sexual promiscuity. Courtship and betrothal lend themselves to the dangers of short-circuiting potential relationships by zealous (if naïve) Christians committed to not date until they find "the one"—which often never happens because their search criteria and rules of interaction are so stringent. Or, as Douglas Wilson alluded, the excessive involvement of parents can kill relationships due to unreasonable biases or unbiblical, unwarranted parental fears. Alternatively, a marital commitment might be made before the couple has time to learn how the other ticks. No one method, then, is bulletproof.

Courtship and dating proponents differ on the merits of activities such as the prom or homecoming. Behind these differences are different sets of assumptions. Courtship and betrothal proponents believe such activities either prematurely whet appetites that ought not be whet or else lead to the formation of unacceptable and dangerous "platonic relationships." They see problems more than opportunities. In contrast, dating proponents would argue that such activities do not necessarily arouse unhealthy or ungodly appetites. They see opportunities more than problems.

But the "problems versus opportunities" trade-off reaches beyond high school dances. For example, a woman might assume a man has a significant, exclusive interest in her if he invites her out for coffee just to casually get to know her. In reading too much into the invitation, she may either gladly accept, only to be disappointed later because her expectations weren't met, or decline the opportunity because she deemed it more serious than was intended. In the case of the former, she may drive the man away by expecting too much. In the case of the latter, she misses the chance to make a better acquaintance by assuming he expected too much.[13] Likewise, a man might think a woman is flirting with him simply because she has a more outgoing personality than he does. In both cases, each is reading the behavior of the other on the basis of his or her set of relational presuppositions.

One principle I hope you will gain from this book is that regardless of where you find yourself on the emotional vulnerability continuum, you have an opportunity to display Christian maturity. We should seek, to the extent possible, to live in such a way that we do not cause our brothers and sisters to stumble. This means that some should curtail their behavior so as not to send false signals. Many guys are notorious for being clueless as to how their forward behavior is rightly being interpreted by women, while just as many women are clueless as to what their outfits and conversations communicate. Likewise, others should seek God's help and the wisdom of older believers to become less susceptible to emotional false alarms. God has obviously wired all of us differently, and we should relate to each other with understanding.

Finally, it is my hope and prayer that whether you date, court, are betrothed, or even are arranged, you would do everything to the glory of God. I close with the most important area of agreement among all five contributors: Relationships, including marriage, are not ultimate but secondary to a relationship with God. They ought to point beyond us to the surpassing glory of being known and loved by the God of the universe who is our Father. In our singleness and marriages, I pray we demonstrate that we truly are captivated with our heavenly Bridegroom and belong above all to Him.

A BIRD'S-EYE VIEW OF THIS BOOK'S ORGANIZATION

ppendix

Alex Chediak

IN ORGANIZING A BOOK SUCH AS THIS ONE, IT WAS CLEAR FROM THE beginning that not every view could be represented. No two authors think identically on this issue. Therefore, contributors were selected based on their views being readily distinguishable from one another. Covering the main spectrum of views held in the Western Christian community was also of paramount importance.

That said, I recognize that each of the five views represented here actually can have multiple shades and nuances. For example, there are a variety of perspectives within the larger category of dating. They differ on the relative value—or danger—associated with casual dating and dating by teenagers, the extent to which group dating should be utilized as an initial step for better acquaintance, and the level of importance that should be placed on Christian community (or society in general).

Likewise, a variety of perspectives are also represented within courtship literature. Some are firmer than others with respect to the authority of the father, the dangers of emotional ties developing between noncommitted partners, the extent to which concerns for purity should limit physical displays of affection, and the importance of age, financial readiness, and male/female relational and vocational roles. For example, with respect to relational roles, courtship proponents would require varying degrees of certainty on the part of the man when he approaches the girl and/or her father. Some would say that the man has as much right to terminate a courtship as the woman. Others suggest he can only legitimately back out if she shows herself to have extreme moral shortcomings. With respect to vocational roles, some proponents would maintain that the man must have a steady job, such that he could immediately support a wife. Such thinking presupposes a complementarian view of marriage.[1]

It's also important for Western Christians to be aware that much of the world follows the custom of arranged marriages. Though an arranged marriage view is not included in this book, a betrothal view is presented—a view that more than any other approximates the arranged marriage situation.

The following continuum, from betrothal to dating, provides a useful way to compare the views represented in this book:

← *Betrothal* 　　　　　　 *Courtship* 　　　　　　 *Dating* →

← Greater preliminary formality 　　　 Less preliminary formality →

← Initial commitment important 　　 Initial commitment less important →

← Damage inevitable 　　　　　　 Damage not inevitable in
　in multiple experiences 　　　　　 in multiple experiences →

← Method more important than culture 　　　 Neutrality of culture →

← Consider objective criteria 　　　 Consider subjective criteria →

As the continuum shows, differences fall into these categories: preliminary formality, initial commitment, preventing relational damage, method versus culture, and objective versus subjective criteria.

Preliminary formality. On the dating side of the spectrum, there can be a high degree of preliminary informality. A couple just getting to know each other is free to have coffee or attend a sporting event, for example. As you move left along the continuum, there is more formality required from the very beginning of the relationship. For example, in courtship, the man is expected to have had a prior conversation with the woman's father regarding the relationship. In betrothal, the couple must previously commit to marrying each other. Preliminary formality goes hand in hand with the second area: initial commitment.

Initial commitment. When a young man and woman experience initial attraction to each other, how much commitment should be required? In the most extreme version of dating, almost no commitment is necessary. The two are free—and even advised—to begin enjoying time with one another. They need not even be considering the possibility of marriage. On the other hand, on the extreme side of betrothal, total commitment is necessary, the logic being that if two people are going to give their hearts to each other, they ought to commit to eventually marrying one another lest they otherwise hurt one another.[2] Courtship maintains this understanding less fully than the betrothal position. Nevertheless, the trend toward a greater degree of initial commitment is maintained as one proceeds to the betrothal side of the continuum.

Preventing relational damage. Another way of viewing the differences among the approaches is with respect to this question: Is relational damage inevitable when a romantic interaction does not result in marriage? While all parties would stress the importance of maintaining emotional and physical purity, those who lean toward the betrothal side of the continuum are more of the opinion that relational damage is inevitable in the event of a breakup. If the young man and woman succeed at maintaining emotional and physical purity, they have learned the bad habit of guarding themselves in a relationship in which God intended them to exhibit unrestricted vulnerability. This can create intimacy problems in marriage. If they fail, any breakup experience can harden their hearts and result in their seeing the marriage bond as less than permanent. Those who lean toward the dating side of the continuum recognize that while dating presents the possibility of emotional and/or physical promiscuity, such behavior is not inevitable. So to rule out the option of dating with integrity and honor before God is to throw out the baby with the bath water.

Method versus culture. In the Western world, dating is the typical approach to finding a spouse. Those who lean toward the dating side of the continuum believe Christians are at liberty to employ cultural patterns that aren't viewed as inherently sinful, such as dating. In other words, dating proponents are more likely to argue that the Bible doesn't prescribe a "correct method" for moving toward marriage; hence, Christians are free to date provided they do so in a manner that honors Scriptural principles of conduct. Betrothal and courtship proponents are more likely to maintain that the Scriptures, when rightly understood, do prescribe a particular approach to marriage; hence, Christians should employ this method, even if cultural norms are thereby disregarded. Some might even suggest that Western culture *itself* should be altered such that Christians would find betrothal or courtship increasingly practical. Indeed, such models seem to thrive in more tightly knit churches, and those communities essentially function as alternate cultures.

Objective versus subjective criteria. While all the contributors would agree that a Christian should marry only another Christian, the extent to which Christians should consider their emotions is often debated. Is it okay, even prudent, to consider emotional and physical attraction? The priority of emotions is frequently captured by Hollywood—the classic tales of forbidden love between couples who feel deeply for each other but lack societal permission to act. The key question for daters might be, "How do I feel about him or her?" Courtship and betrothal advocates may instead focus on objective or intellectual considerations, such as, "Is he from the right kind of family? Do my parents approve? Do friends think we'd be good together?" Proponents on the betrothal side might even warn against basing life decisions such as marriage on emotional grounds. Meanwhile, those on the dating side of the continuum warn of loveless marriages between people who deep down inside would rather be with someone else. They might also argue that courtship and betrothal lead people to have a checklist approach toward mate selection.

In summary, a final way to understand the continuum is that toward the dating side, it seems one falls in love and then marries. On the betrothal side, one makes a commitment and then falls in love.

NOTES

INTRODUCTION TO THE 5 PATHS

1. Michelle Conlin, "Unmarried America," *Business Week*, October 20, 2003, 106–116.

CHAPTER 1: THE COUNTERCULTURAL PATH

1. Tova Mirvis, *The Outside World* (New York: Knopf, 2004), 13, 19–20.
2. Mirvis, 20.
3. Space limitations make this by necessity a cursory and perhaps oversimplified summary of the history of dating in America. My generalizations best describe the conventions of courting and dating upheld by middle-class, white Protestants. Immigrant communities, in particular, may boast very different social arrangements. My periodization relies on Beth L. Bailey, *From Front Porch to Back Seat: Courtship in Twentieth-Century America* (Baltimore: Johns Hopkins University Press, 1989).
4. Stephanie Coontz, *Marriage, a History: From Obedience to Intimacy or How Love Conquered Marriage* (New York: Viking, 2005); Lois Carr and Lorena Walsh, "The Planter's Wife: The Experience of White Women in Seventeenth-Century Maryland," *William and Mary Quarterly*, 3rd ser., 34 (1977): 542–572; Mary Beth Norton, "The Myth of the Golden Age," in *Women of America: A History*, ed. Carol R. Berkin and Mary Beth Norton, 37–46 (New York: Houghton Mifflin, 1979); Lauren F. Winner, "Material Culture and Anglican Religious Practice in Eighteenth-Century Virginia" (PhD diss., Columbia University, forthcoming).
5. Bailey, 12.
6. Bailey, 15–20.

7. Bailey, 58.

8. Benoit Denizet-Lewis, "Friends, Friends with Benefits and the Benefits of the Local Mall," *The New York Times*, May 30, 2004, http://www.nytimes .com/2004/05/30/magazine/30NONDATING.html.

9. Denizet-Lewis.

10. Joshua Harris, *Boy Meets Girl: Say Hello to Courtship* (Sisters, OR: Multnomah, 2000), 29–38.

11. Contributors to this volume have been asked, among other things, to specifically comment on how the seventh chapter of Paul's first epistle to the Corinthians bears on the question of dating. This chapter is one of the most frequently misinterpreted in all of Paul's letters, and I would suggest that a correct reading of this chapter shows that it does not bear on dating at all. Chapter 7 deals with sex and marriage: Should Corinthian Christians who are already married refrain from sexual relations with their spouses? Should those who are widowed remarry? Should engaged couples go forward with their marriage plans?

In responding to the Corinthians' questions, Paul makes at least two points germane to single people. First, singleness is a state blessed by God. This is something contemporary Christians, especially Protestants, have a hard time hearing. Our society is so sex-saturated and the church has so elevated the nuclear family that we often think of singleness as a second-class state. In 1 Corinthians 7, Paul suggests the opposite — he sanctions marriage, to be sure, but he suggests that singleness is actually a preferable state. Second, people should remain in "the condition in which [they] were called" — that is, if you were married when you first heard the gospel, you should remain married, and if you were unmarried, it is better for you to remain unmarried.

Thus Paul's words bear not at all on the manner in which persons who wish to get married should go about doing so — dating versus courtship versus betrothal. Rather, if we take his words at face value, dating, courtship, and betrothal would all be frowned on because all single people should remain unmarried! Paul urged the Corinthians to remain in "the condition in which [they] were called" because of his eschatology — he expected the Lord to return in his lifetime. Clearly, that did not come to pass; we await Christ's return still.

This does not mean, however, that we are to dismiss those sections of Paul that most clearly reflect an imminent eschatology. We can still take from 1 Corinthians 7 an insight about what it means to live in perpetual readiness for the second coming of Christ. New Testament scholar Richard Hays, for example, suggests that Paul's eschatological framework "enables us to look to the future in trust and hope, knowing that our salvation depends not on our success in restructuring the world but on the vast mercy and justice of God." See Richard B. Hays, *First Corinthians* (Louisville: John Knox Press, 1997), 110–134.

12. For a useful discussion of this point, see Donna Freitas and Jason King, *Save the Date: A Spirituality of Dating, Love, Dinner, and the Divine* (New York: Crossroad, 2003), 50–53.

13. Because all the contributors to this volume agree that Christians are called to chastity, I won't spend much time developing an ethic of chastity here. This section is a brief overview of many themes I develop at length in *Real Sex: The Naked Truth About Chastity* (Grand Rapids, MI: Brazos Press, 2005).

14. These reader reviews can be found online at http://www.amazon.com/gp/ product/customer-reviews/1590521358/ref=cm_cr_dp_2_1/103 -2992580-4030220?%5Fencoding=UTF8&customer-reviews.sort%5Fby= -SubmissionDate&n=283155.

15. Casey Moss, quoted in Laurie Goodstein, "New Christian Take on the Old Dating Ritual," *The New York Times*, September 9, 2001.

16. Diogenes Allen, *Love: Christian Romance, Marriage, Friendship* (Cambridge, MA: Cowley Publications, 1987), 30.

17. Søren Kierkegaard, *Works of Love*, quoted in Amy Laura Hall, *Kierkegaard and the Treachery of Love* (New York: Cambridge University Press, 1998), 111.

18. Wendy Shalit, *A Return to Modesty: Discovering the Lost Virtue* (New York: Free Press, 1999), 31.

19. Allen, 28–29.

20. Søren Kierkegaard, *Works of Love*, trans. and ed. Howard V. Hong and Edna H. Hong (Princeton, NJ: Princeton University Press, 1995), 164.

21. Hall, 87, 112, 173, passim.

22. Søren Kierkegaard, *Works of Love*, 149, quoted in Hall, 188.

23. Hall, 101–102, 111.

24. Hall, 188–199.

25. Allen, 67, 84.

26. David Matzko McCarthy, *The Good Life: Genuine Christianity for the Middle Class* (Grand Rapids, MI: Brazos Press, 2004), 61.

27. See Tim Keller's series of tapes, "Sex, Singleness, and Marriage," which can be found on the website of Redeemer Presbyterian Church, New York, New York, http://www.redeemer2.com/resources/index.cfm?fuseaction=media.

28. Denizet-Lewis.

29. Lauren Winner, "Solitary Refinement," *Christianity Today*, June 11, 2001, http://www.christianitytoday.com/ct/2001/008/1.30.html; Lana Trent et al., *Single and Content* (Dallas: Word, 1999).

CHAPTER 2: THE COURTSHIP PATH

1. William Shakespeare, *Much Ado About Nothing*, act II, scene iii, line 214.

2. All Scripture quotations in this chapter are taken from the *New King James Version* (NKJV).

CHAPTER 3: THE GUIDED PATH

1. See Douglas Wilson, *Her Hand in Marriage: Biblical Courtship in the Modern World* (Moscow, ID: Canon Press, 1997); Josh Harris, *I Kissed Dating Goodbye: A New Attitude Toward Romance and Relationships* (Sisters, OR: Multnomah, 1997) and *Boy Meets Girl: Say Hello to Courtship* (Sisters, OR: Multnomah, 2000); and Paul Jehle, *Dating vs. Courtship* (Plymouth, MA: Plymouth Rock Foundation, 2001).

2. Unless otherwise identified, all Scripture quotations in this chapter are taken from the *English Standard Version* (ESV).

3. Jehle, 113. Note Jehle's assertion about the Isaac and Rebekah narrative: "In principle it is an *authoritative* guide for us to follow" (emphasis added).

4. One example is Eric and Leslie Ludy, *When God Writes Your Love Story* (Sisters, OR: Loyal Publishing, 1999). The Ludys have an encouraging

story and share lots of good advice. But though their book includes some applicable biblical texts, it is made up predominately of stories that warm the heart but carry no scriptural authority.

5. Harris, *Boy Meets Girl*, 32.

6. Wilson, 83.

7. Ravi Zacharias, *I, Isaac, Take Thee, Rebekah: Moving from Romance to Lasting Love* (Nashville: W Publishing, 2004), 22.

8. For a helpful discussion about obeying and disobeying parents regarding whom to marry, see J. Douma, *The Ten Commandments: Manual for the Christian Life* (Phillipsburg, NJ: P & R Publishing, 1996), 174–175.

9. John Piper, "A Vision of Complementarity" in *Recovering Biblical Manhood and Womanhood*, eds. John Piper and Wayne Grudem (Wheaton, IL: Crossway, 1991), 33.

10. Piper, 35–36.

11. A helpful resource for learning about marriage is Wayne Mack's *Preparing for Marriage God's Way* (Tulsa, OK: Virgil Hensley Publishing, 1986).

12. D. Edmond Hiebert, *1 & 2 Thessalonians* (Chicago: Moody, 1992), 184.

13. Leon Morris, cited in Hiebert, 186.

14. Anthony C. Thiselton, *The New International Greek Testament Commentary: The First Epistle to the Corinthians* (Grand Rapids, MI: Eerdmans, 2000), 498–501.

CHAPTER 4: THE BETROTHAL PATH

1. Unless otherwise identified, all Scripture quotations in this chapter are taken from the *New King James Version* (NKJV).

2. Paul's reference to a man and "his virgin" in 1 Corinthians 7:36-38 is apparently a reference to either the father or the bridegroom of a betrothed woman.

3. On the basis of this principle in Deuteronomy 22:28-29, some singles might intentionally enter into a fornication relationship, assuming this would require a subsequent marriage. The Lord provides an interesting clarification in Exodus 22:16-17. He specifically says, "If a man entices a virgin who is not betrothed, and lies with her, he shall surely pay the bride-price for her to be his wife. If her father utterly refuses to give her to him, he shall pay money according to the bride-price of virgins."

While there was no requirement of being put to death, as in the case of illicit relations for a married person (adultery), such immorality between single people (fornication) required the young man to pay the bride-price and marry her, but only if her father so allowed. If her father didn't allow them to get married, the man still had to pay the bride-price ("because he has humbled her," Deuteronomy 22:29), but he didn't get the bride.

4. *American Dictionary of the English Language*, s.v. "Shamefacedness."

CHAPTER 5: THE PURPOSEFUL PATH

1. Jeramy Clark, *I Gave Dating a Chance* (Colorado Springs, CO: WaterBrook, 2004), 15.

2. *Random House Webster's Collegiate Dictionary*, 2nd ed., s.v. "Date."

3. Unless otherwise identified, all Scripture quotations in this chapter are taken from *The New International Version* (NIV).

4. Stuart Briscoe, "Luxuries, or Necessities?," *Men's Devotional Bible* (Grand Rapids, MI: Zondervan, 1993), 1380.

5. Shirley Rice, *The Christian Home: A Woman's View* (Norfolk, VA: Norfolk Christian Schools, 1965), lesson 3.

6. C. S. Lewis, "First and Second Things," in *First and Second Things: Essays on Theology and Ethics*, ed. Walter Hooper (London: HarperCollins, 1985).

7. Millard J. Erickson, *Christian Theology* (Grand Rapids, MI: Baker, 1983), 866.

8. Dr. Richard Mayhue, "Comforter or Helper?," (handout, pneumatology class at The Master's Seminary, Sun Valley, CA, 1995).

9. James Dobson, *What Wives Wish Their Husbands Knew About Women* (Wheaton, IL: Tyndale, 1979), 91.

10. Roy Hession, *The Calvary Road*, rev. ed. (Fort Washington, PA: Christian Literature Crusade, 2000), 55.

11. Anonymous quote inscribed on the wall of the National Archives in Washington, D.C.

12. Clark, *I Gave Dating a Chance*, 106.

13. H. Norman Wright and Wes Roberts, *Before You Say "I Do"* (Eugene, OR: Harvest House, 1978), 54.

14. Jeramy and Jerusha Clark, *Define the Relationship* (Colorado Springs, CO: WaterBrook, 2004), 27–28.
15. Clark, *I Gave Dating a Chance*, 49.
16. *Random House Webster's Collegiate Dictionary*, 2nd ed., s.v. "Erode."

CONCLUSION: HOW THIS ALL COMES TOGETHER

1. See, for example, the article from *The New York Times* that Lauren Winner referenced.
2. Lev Grossman, "Grow Up? Not So Fast," *Time*, January 24, 2005, 42–54; U.S. Bureau of the Census, September 15, 2004, http://www.census.gov/population/socdemo/hh-fam/tabMS-2.pdf.
3. Michelle Conlin, "Unmarried America," *Business Week*, October 20, 2003, 106–116.
4. Andrew Witmer and Ken Myers, *Wandering Toward the Altar: The Decline of American Courtship* (audiocassette), Mars Hill Audio, 2000.
5. Douglas LeBlanc, "Affectionate Patriarchs: An Interview with W. Bradford Wilcox" *Christianity Today*, August 2004, 44. This article can also be accessed at http://www.christianitytoday.com/ct/2004/008/26.44.html.
6. Ronald J. Sider, "The Scandal of the Evangelical Conscience" *Christianity Today*, January/February 2005, http://www.christianitytoday.com/bc/2005/001/3.8.html.
7. Albert Mohler, "Deliberate Childlessness: Moral Rebellion with a New Face," *crosswalk.com*, June 28, 2004, http://www.crosswalk.com/news/weblogs/mohler/?adate=6/28/2004#1270710.
8. LeBlanc, 44.
9. I do recognize the legitimacy of some couples temporarily delaying having children due to severe financial restrictions. I am speaking here of an *attitude* some bring to marriage that precludes part of the reason God established the institution.
10. All Scripture quotations in the conclusion are taken from the *New King James Version* (NKJV).
11. I am aware that many single Christian women are eager to marry and have children. For you, an application might be as follows: (a) Be

content, fighting the temptation to fall into self-pity and rejoicing in your love affair with God; (b) Recognize that significance is bestowed by God, not by your marital status; (c) Pursue Christian community and service with the kinds of Christians among whom God may reveal a quality mate; (d) Consider only men who are worthy of your respect, but be realistic (not idealistic) in your expectations; (e) Lastly, be a blessing to those around you, using your singleness to serve others and prepare for marriage by developing hospitality. I would highly commend to you *The Rich Single Life* by Andy Farmer and *Did I Kiss Marriage Goodbye?* by Carolyn McCulley.

12. Douglas Wilson, *Reforming Marriage* (Moscow, ID: Canon Press, 1995).

13. For more on this dilemma, see Rob Marcus, "Kissing Nonsense Goodbye," *Christianity Today*, June 11, 2001, 46.

APPENDIX: A BIRD'S-EYE VIEW OF THIS BOOK'S ORGANIZATION

1. Egalitarians believe a husband and wife are to submit to one another *in the same way* in a marriage. Complementarians believe they are to submit to each other *differently* in a marriage. In the latter view, the husband is the God-ordained leader, and the wife is the follower. This often implies that the man is expected to take initiative and responsibility for the relationship itself, whereas such duties can seemingly be more or less equally divided in the egalitarian model. (One can also discuss role distinctions, or a lack thereof, in local churches, but that topic is beyond the scope of this book.)

2. However, as the dating views represented here are Christian dating views, it is understood that some commitment is inherently present in every opposite-sex interaction—namely, Christians are always under the moral statutes expressly presented in the Scriptures. Therefore, letting them "try things out" does not mean they are at liberty to experiment sexually. Nevertheless, dating proponents place less stress on the need for initial commitment than betrothal proponents. Those who hold to other views fall in between, as represented by the continuum.

AUTHORS

ALEX CHEDIAK has been involved in lay ministry with singles of all ages in capacities ranging from summer camps to preaching and teaching. Most recently, he was a pastoral intern at Grace Community Church in Gardnerville, Nevada, where he delivered a series of messages on singleness, romance, and biblical wisdom to a multigenerational congregation. These messages will be delineated in a forthcoming book with Christian Focus Publishers. In the fall of 2005, he will be an apprentice at The Bethlehem Institute under Dr. John Piper. He plans to pursue a ministry aimed at church-based adult Christian education and training, building bridges between seminaries and churches and writing on culturally relevant topics from a God-centered perspective. Recently married, Alex and his wife, Marni, reside in Eagan, Minnesota.

LAUREN F. WINNER is the author of *Girl Meets God: A Memoir*, *Mudhouse Sabbath*, and *Real Sex: The Naked Truth About Chastity*. *Girl Meets God* was selected for the Discover Great New Writers program at Barnes & Noble and won the Logos award for Best Book on Christianity and Culture. Lauren is a contributing editor to *Christianity Today* magazine and has written for periodicals ranging from *Books and Culture: A Christian Review* to *The New York Times Book Review*. She and her husband, Griff, live in Virginia.

DOUGLAS WILSON is a senior fellow of theology at New St. Andrews College. He has written multiple books, including *Recovering the Lost Tools of Learning*, *Reforming Marriage*, *Her Hand in Marriage*, and *Mother Kirk*. He is the editor of the bimonthly magazine *Credenda/Agenda* and is one of the founders of Logos School in Moscow, Idaho. Douglas is a frequent speaker at conferences dealing with Christian education, where he often addresses the topics of masculinity, femininity, dating, and courtship. Douglas has been married for twenty-seven years. He and his wife, Nancy, have three grown children and nine grandchildren.

DR. RICK HOLLAND is the pastor of College and Student Ministries at Grace Community Church in Sun Valley, California, and an instructor at The Master's College and Seminary. Rick is a regular conference speaker, both nationally and internationally, and preaches weekly to a ministry of over one thousand collegians. His essay in this volume is a snapshot of a book he is writing on romance and relationships. Rick and his wife, Kim, have three sons.

JONATHAN LINDVALL and his wife, Connie, have been married since 1976 and homeschool their six children in Springville, California. Jonathan is president of Bold Christian Living and administrator of Christian Pilgrims Schools, International, a homeschool ministry. He speaks at various conferences and presents Bold Christian Youth Seminars and Bold Parenting Seminars, as well as the New Testament House Church Seminar in the U.S. and internationally. His focus is on the relationship between godly families and New Testament churches.

JERAMY AND JERUSHA CLARK have served in youth ministry for a combined twenty years. After meeting at The First Evangelical Free

Church of Fullerton, where the Clarks both served in youth ministry, they moved to Monument, Colorado, where they ministered at Tri-Lakes Chapel. Currently, Jeramy, Jerusha, and their two children live in Escondido, California, where Jeramy pastors five hundred high school students at Emmanuel Faith Community Church. They are the coauthors of *After You Drop Them Off: A Parent's Guide to Student Ministry* and three books on relationships: *I Gave Dating a Chance; He's HOT, She's HOT;* and *DTR: Define the Relationship.*

> If you've found this book helpful, or even if you haven't, Alex Chediak would love to hear your thoughts. Please feel free to write him at 5paths@gmail.com or drop by http://www.geocities.com/fivepaths/.

OWN YOUR FAITH.